LETTERS FROM THE BELL TOWER

A collection of poetry, prose,
and personal philosophy.

From the heart, soul, and mind of:
Clyde R. Hurlston

On behalf of the author, thank you for your purchase.
And may The Hermetic Principles guide us all.

www.clydehurlston.com
facebook.com/adebtpaidinink
@adebtpaidinink

"QUASIMODO" ART BY BOWIE

"He therefore turned to mankind only with regret. His cathedral was enough for him. It was peopled with marble figures of kings, saints and bishops who at least did not laugh in his face and looked at him with only tranquillity and benevolence. The other statues, those of monsters and demons, had no hatred for him – he resembled them too closely for that. It was rather the rest of mankind that they jeered at. The saints were his friends and blessed him; the monsters were his friends and kept watch over him. He would sometimes spend whole hours crouched before one of the statues in solitary conversation with it. If anyone came upon him, then he would run away like a lover surprised during a serenade."

- Victor Hugo, The Hunchback of Notre-Dame

I
RELATIONS

"Love is like a friendship caught on fire. In the beginning a flame, very pretty, often hot and fierce, but still only light and flickering. As love grows older, our hearts mature and our love becomes as coals, deep-burning and unquenchable."

- Bruce Lee

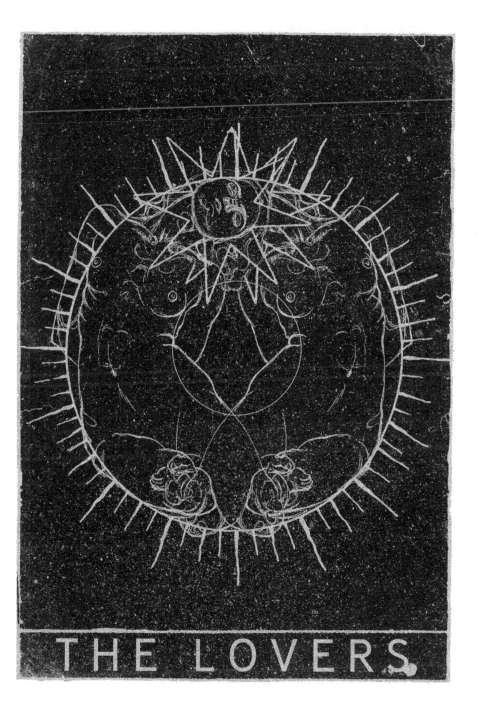

READY? AIM. FIRE!

She once told me that the difference between wanting and needing was merely the passage of time.

As each tick of the second hand sounded like cannons in her subconscious, she knew the more she stared at my face, the slower my hands would move.

And with each minute that dies, she becomes mine.

First in body, then I will eventually penetrate and reach her soul. Because deep down I knew, this is how she likes it. Movement at a snail's pace, but a passion fueled with the intensity of war. On this night, victory shall come; along with both of us... but at a price.

No one will walk away unscathed. There will be no amicable splits. After tonight, there will be no "just friends" mantras recited. After dams give way to the rivers of her love, and after my weapon of choice has exploded and covered this battlefield in a joy withheld...

How on Earth will we be able to do anything except look at each other every night henceforth and whisper,

"Ready? Aim. Fire!"

DROWNING IN LUST

Would it be forward of me,
To demand your presence here?
I've grown tired of my hands,
Having to suffice with dreams.
Don't you see?
I want to drown my loneliness with lust.
I want to drink from your fountain,
Until we both need to come up for air.
I want to search the valleys for your peaks.
I want to punish your garden,
Until I can feel your soul from the inside.
I want to feel as your fingertips
Make their beds within my back,
Until I paint my masterpiece upon your temple walls.
I want to become your need.
Oh, darling...
I want your preferred methods of pleasure,
To be the only ways I know.
God damn it, don't you see?
I want to stop wanting.
I want to start feeling.
Won't you return to me?
Be my dream while I'm awake for once.

CRAVING SILENCE

What is it about silence?
Why does the space between sounds,
Give us so much room to think?
So much room to crave?
Well, I have spent this quiet time reflecting.
And as the moon dances on the water's face,
I wonder about you.
I'm wondering: where you are...
How do you feel? And, are you craving me?
But then the doubts creep in,
They come to me like shadows.
Knowing that silence is their sunset.
The time when their influence is most powerful.
They tell me such hurtful things.
They say you are well, but you are not alone.
And the things that you now crave,
Are not possessed by me.
They say that is the reason for your silence.
But the truth is, shadows lie.
They lie right to my face.
I could walk straight into the sun, and they would tell
you that I was going the other way.
But in the end, I'm lying too.
I'm lying here...
Alone. Silent. And craving you.

MIRACULOUS

I once spoke in whispers,
While others spoke in tongues.
But desire choked the breath,
That sought to fill my lungs.
What's the meaning of existence,
If we must deny our needs?
When our minds are fertile ground,
For temptation's wicked seeds.
Buried deep beneath our shame,
Lies the source of human guilt.
And mine was surely sacrificed,
Upon the altar that I built.
But still, some people walk on water,
While others drown on land.
And there are so many things,
That I will never understand.
Like how all the pretty roses,
Always overlook the vines.
And if Christ turned water into wine,
Why can't I make her mine?
When I have witnessed resurrections,
And I have witnessed crimes.
But it seems my feelings of surprise,
Are a victim of the times.
Darling, have you ever wondered
What makes the world go 'round?
Or is it only worship,
That gets your knees upon the ground?

THE SUBTLE TOUCH OF FATE

She was once like a paper doll...
Fragile. Magnificent.
Something worthy of being carefully held,
And then proudly displayed.
She was folded into her current shape,
By the cruelest of circumstances.
Or as I like to call it,
The subtle touch of fate.
She was gradually hardened by experience.
Yet, still remained soft beneath her armor.
Though you wouldn't know that,
Unless she let you get close enough to touch.
But if you weren't careful,
It would be you that would suffer the consequences.
And if you looked closely, you would see,
That you stopped moving way back there.
For that is your blood making love to the ground;
Not hers.

SAMSON'S HANDS

Patience is a virtue, and virtues are for saints.
All I have here for you, my love
Is a laundry list of my complaints.
But I won't bore us both with those
No, I'd rather hold my breath.
While watching paint dry upon the walls
And other slower forms of death.
But there I go, the rambling man
Do I love to hear me speak?
Or do I love the strength I've come to find,
Each time you're feeling weak?
And now my craziness has become aroused
When you stand defiant of my demands.
For it makes me want to bring this temple down,
As if I had the strength of Samson's hands.
But I guess this is all my fucking fault anyway...
Isn't that right, Delilah?

SUBCONSCIOUS RENAISSANCE

I have visions with my eyes closed.
Sometimes, I shut them so tightly,
That I begin to see colors.
They swirl and pool; collide and crash.
Until they combine
And begin to paint the image of your face.
Even in true darkness, you are radiant.
Darling,
Do you even know how beautiful you are?
Do you even know what you do to me?
I swear, it's not fair.
How are you at the center of my subconscious
renaissance, when I am nothing to you?
I guess I'll never know the reasons.
But the proof is in the blackness.
And I am waiting there for you.

FASHION THE VINES

I once felt much closer to Heaven,
Than I ever had before.
But you pulled the metaphoric rug,
And sent me crashing to the floor.
I never did venture to guess,
Just exactly why you chose
To fashion the vines into a noose
That you quickly slipped on to the rose.
And as its stem was searching for the ground,
As if the chair had fallen down
You weren't even the slightest bit concerned
Nor did you even make a sound.
No, you witnessed fabled thorns begin to dull,
As the precious petals cried their red.
And I hoped they would cry enough
To drown the bitter memories,
That you once engraved into my head.

INTERNAL COMPASS

Oh, my internal compass
Keeps pointing straight to you.
And that direction would be displayed,
Until the day was through.
But I have found the inner strength,
To turn the navigation off.
And now I just remind myself,
That I am far from lost.
'Cause I've been down that road enough,
To know exactly where it leads.
So I don't have to stop and guess,
Or even find a sign to read.
'Cause in your premature departure,
An opportunity arose.
For me to open up a hidden door
Once tightly sealed and closed.
And with a little luck I freed,
This sweet perspective from its cage.
And as it climbed into the sky,
I felt it dissipate the rage.
Which once had kept it shackled,
And so restrained from flight.
But now, if you didn't speak too loud
You could hear its cries of joy at night.

CASTING SHADOWS

The deception of perception
Cast shadows on a point of view
But I'd rather throw these sharpened blades,
If I want to make a point or two.
Hit or miss, my little priss
You should cover up your better parts.
For spades often pierce the diamonds of,
Those in possession of the weaker hearts.
But please give my regards to your cards,
It seems you went and played them well.
Yet I'm laughing while I'm whispering,
The only tale I ever want to tell.
It sucks to be you, and it sucks to be me.
If we can find another imbecile,
I will carve a line through all three.
"Here lies tic, tac, and toe.
They tried their best, but had to go."
Is what the tombstone will read,
After the pastor does his show.
But I would much rather be turned to ash,
And stuffed inside a jar.
That way if you'd need another line,
You wouldn't have to reach as far.
The way you did when I still lived,
And you pretended that you care.
Excuse me while I go down with Kamikaze style,
For once displaying a little flair.

SIGNED, THE MUSEUM PATRON

My mind is a museum,
And sadly, you are behind the glass.
A treasure discovered long ago by my eyes.
My, how you have left them wide with wonder.
Yet I am sad to report,
That visiting hours are only when my eyes are closed.
Darling, that is when I dream of you.
But I can never touch you,
I can never taste you.
Your love will never decorate my lips.
For you are magnificent.
And worse yet, you don't belong to me.
Oh baby, will it ever be my turn?

HELIOCENTRIC LOVE

You are the sun. I am a lonely, city street.
Walked on, neglected. Driven madly.
But no one even remembers I am here.
Unless I become an inconvenience.
But not you. You warm me with just a look.
Oh, if only you knew what you do to me.
I could melt here beneath your glow,
And proudly become your blackened sea.
But I know I'm not supposed to stare at you.
They say it's bad for my eyes.
Yet, I'm already blind, darling.
Blind to every thing and everyone.
That doesn't look like you.
They are but candles, when compared to you.
For as I said, you are the sun, my love.
And as I lie here waiting,
With bated breath I wonder...
When the dark clouds finally part,
Will you return to me?

STARRY NIGHT

Here I am again, in that all too familiar place.
Violently washed ashore, as another sliver of hope
Has capsized into my reservoir of words.
And as I lie breathless and tattered,
The wonders of this starry night are reflected upon the
darkened face, of these still waters that run deep.
I pretend that each star was a wish I made in vain;
For there was a child behind my eyes, who never knew that
the cost always came before the gain.
But the light from those stars came too late;
Just like the wisdom I retained,
After learning lessons from the pain.
Darling, it fucking kills me to know
You'll never be mine again.
The messages in these bottles will never reach your shore.
No, they'll just eventually be taken by the waves.
Proving that our expectations
Turn out to be dark, yet shallow graves.
The places where our childish dreams go to die.

CONFESSIONS OF A MARTYR

I was once a martyr.
Dying on an unseen cross,
For the sins of other men.
My hope for love was lashed,
And left bleeding in the sand.
My motives were labeled blasphemous.
My charity with good will and compliments,
Were labeled as the acts of a charlatan.
I was "too good to be true," they said.
But then I was betrayed.
Not with a kiss on the cheek;
But rather an "Aww, that's sweet" shaped spear
That was plunged into my side.
There were no thirty pieces of silver left for them.
Just the realization that they were now Pilate,
Inside of eyes that once saw them as golden.
The good in a man died that day.
And they went on to love their respective Judas.
While I was surprisingly resurrected,
Both bitter and alone.

BRAVE THE LABYRINTH

To some, courting is a game.
But to me, it has been a maze.
A labyrinth.
One in which, I have run into many dead ends.
Along with unforgiving walls.
That knowingly block my progress,
And impede my travels.
Stopping me from reaching the greatest prize
That I have ever known.
I hear them mock me, as I turn around to start again.
But still, I traverse the maze.
Always hoping to find my way to her.
And yet, I must be honest.
My last time in this maze nearly crushed my will forever.
But today, I've decided to give it another try.
Maybe this time will be the charm.
Or maybe this time, will finally be the end of me.
Either way,
She is truly worth the risk.

PRIZED COLLECTIONS

Here you are, lying in my bed.
Laying on your side,
The pillows look like clouds beneath your head.
You are asleep; ever so soundly.
But me? I'm wide awake.
I can't sleep, baby.
I won't avert my eyes again.
After everything we have done tonight,
I may never sleep the same.
Here, as I'm lying beside you…
I am at peace.
I have been to Heaven and back,
And yet, I've never left this bed.
The things I have witnessed tonight,
Have stolen prized collections of my breath.
And the things that you have done,
Have introduced my fears to death.
Darling, how can I every repay you?

SCORCHED EARTH

You could never tell I suffer well,
If you stared at my facade.
Knowing that my lovers often disappear,
Are they not a cruel mirage?
Yet expectations help us seep the air,
Out of both loving lungs and throat
Helping the windows to our souls,
Be surrounded by these bitter moats.
But now I'm digging past the love
To find the hate that they deserve.
And I'll bury all these memories that,
I had been fighting to preserve.
So I'll find comfort in the fantasies,
And the double lives we've led.
Then I'll watch them as they suffocate,
On these words they've never said.
Then we'll pretend the slate is clean,
Although our hands are not.
As we scorch the entire Earth,
In the hopes of killing truths,
We've left in the angry sun to rot.

MY LYING HEART

Today, I am feeling overwhelmed.
My eyes burn, but fail to cry.
My breaths? Short and to the point.
And I feel as though, I am drowning on land.
I never was much good at swimming, though.
Yet, I want to put on the brave face.
I want to tell the world I'm fine.
But I was never much good at lying.
So I just sit here.
A blank stare from a blank slate.
Reflecting flashes from the family screen.
Searching the ocean in my mind,
Trying to find the words to say.
But I never was much good at talking.
I don't know what I'm good for anymore.
All I know,
Is that I wish she would walk through that door.
So she could kiss me,
And tell me that he was going to be alright.
Because maybe I would believe her.
And not my lying heart.

STONES MADE TO FALL

I am a terrible liar.
I feign and pretend to be cold to you,
Knowing that you know I am full of it.
How can someone so verbose,
Suddenly become a mute?
How can a master of endless, run-on sentences
Suddenly stoop to the level of one word answers.
I'll tell you how, darling... Restraint.
I'm trying to rebuild the walls.
Of the dam you brought down.
Trying in vain,
To restrain an ocean of emotions,
That neither of us were prepared to face.
It's why I've tried to avoid you at all costs.
One glance, one whisper, and down they come again.
The stones fall like raindrops.
Crashing down upon my house of cards.
And yes, I know what I said.
I said that I had finally moved on.
But that was a lie.
Darling, you've raised the bar so high,
How could I ever get over you?
I can't.
And so, I just keep on pretending,
That I'm not still trying to reach you.

RESERVOIR OF WORDS

On the surface, she was safe.
Barely dipping her toes into my mind.
My hidden reservoir of words.
She said it seemed lovely, dark, and deep.
Like the woods Robert Frost once spoke of.
"Did you hear me, Demi?"
On the surface, she was safe.
Knowing she could wave her hand
Across the water's face,
And see only her reflection.
No other moon lit my face the way that she did.
But she was too scared to dive in.
Afraid of being overwhelmed and drowned.
No longer belonging to herself.
But to be completely mine.
Until my voice rang in her ears
Like the little birds Bob Marley once sang of.
Until my compliments tumbled through her veins.
Until my fingerprints made mosaics,
On the finest frame I have ever pictured.
Such splendor, darling.
Won't you join me here? In the abyss.
I promise, there are wonders to behold.
So come home to me.
Before my shoulder starts turning cold.

FRANKLY UNINVITED

I'm going to be frank with you...
I'm tired of this shit.
The wanting you, the needing you,
The never getting you.
This shit needs to stop.
I'm not asking for forever, baby.
For fuck's sake, just once.
Just once in my life, I want to get
The thing I want the most.
And what I want is you.
So why can't I have you?
I'm mean fuck, look around.
In this world,
Cowards get to live far longer than heroes.
The greedy get to feed their avarice.
And what do I get? Nothing.
Just dreams. Dreams of you...
Dreams that are so fucking hot,
They leave smoke in my subconscious.
I'm tired of not being able to breathe.
I'm tired of staring through the museum glass.
I'm tired of being unchosen.
I'm fucking incredible in my own right.
And it's about goddamn time you opened your eyes.
To really let them see me properly.
Just once.
Not forever... just once.
Just once lay before me, and let me worship you.
Then be brave enough to endure
A little over three decades worth
Of both pleasure and punishment.
All in one night.
Like catching a hurricane in a bottle.
Oh baby, you're making me hate you.
And all I want to do is love you.
But I can't go, where I'm not invited.

HELLO, MOTHER LION.

As I write this I'm sitting here,
Surrounded by friends and loved ones.
I should be content.
And I am... for the most part.
But I must admit, I feel the slightest sting of loneliness.
And it makes me wonder...
How are you, Mother Lion?
How is your little cub?
Have you run across the plains as of late?
With all of your strength and majesty on display?
Others seeking attention,
For what just comes naturally to you.
You are so incredible.
Breathtaking to witness in your element.
And I have never even seen you up close.
But I want to. I want it so badly.
I know the risks; I know how dangerous it could be.
But I want to meet you anyway.
And fear not, Mother Lion.
I would never want to tame you.
No, my dear...
I just want to run wild beside you.
As your King.

DEHYDRATED HEARTS

I am so tired of trying,
My profound efforts wasted in vain.
Knowing people will fear the floods,
And still they pray for rain.
Must we continue on this course?
Must we play our parts?
On this stage we've labeled life,
That stars our dehydrated hearts.
But as the curtains close today,
Making room for night.
I have had a bone to pick,
That I must now bring to light.
What can be said about a person,
Who ignites a spark within a soul?
Then keeps stoking all the flames,
Until they rage out of control.
But when the smoke gives them a warning,
They surely run toward the hills.
While running across bridges set alight,
For the sake of their fleeting thrills.
To me, they are the cowards
With life's hardest lessons to be learned.
For if you cause a fire inside of me,
You had best be set to burn.
Otherwise,
I will dance in the ashes of your mind.

FOR YOU, BELOVED

Oh, my Beloved,
Once wrongly labeled as a spider...
You aren't the source of my pain.
And apologies aren't necessary,
When the partcipants were willing.
And let's be honest, when I had you,
I was ill-prepared and couldn't even handle you.
What a sad sight I must have been.
And come to think of it,
I was only removed from my shell
By your passion and your grace.
And it kills me that I couldn't reciprocate it,
In a fashion that you deserved.
Still, with you, I was a King for the night
And a martyr for the hours.
But I never made you feel like a Queen.
Or the Goddess that you are.
Nowadays, my hunger for you is still there.
Primarily fueled by my inability to have you.
Along with the fumes of memories,
And the pain of knowing
I was such a disaster in your bed.
I wasn't a king. I was a frightened, young man
Who had no business being inside of you.
Since I hadn't earned my place.
And for that, I am truly sorry.

- *For Natalie*

MADE FOR PLASTIC CUPS

I wanted to tell you something beautiful today,
But I didn't get to hear your voice.
That has sadly become a pattern as of late.
Life keeps giving us far more than we can handle,
And forgetting to leave the receipts upon our dressers.
But we'll make do, and keep the darkness at bay.
We don't have a choice, we're just wired that way.
But darling, what I wanted to tell you is this...
I miss you. Rather, I miss you terribly.
No hyperbole. No exaggeration. Just truth.
Keeping the promise that I made to you.
And the truth is, I feel lost when I don't hear from you.
I'm sorry if I overwhelm you with my affections.
I have a bad habit of hiding oceans behind my eyes,
And then trying to fit waterfalls inside of plastic cups.
The poor things weren't made to handle all of this.
But I feel as though, you were made for me.
And I have waited thirty plus years,
For someone as incredible as you.
Yet, I feel as though you're slipping through my fingers.
And I only want to hold you,
For as long as I've waited for you.
Is that so much to ask?
I've never been this close to glory before.
And I need to know if you really exist.
Because you are beginning to feel,
Like a figment of my cruel imagination.

HEARTFELT THUNDERSTORMS

They say bad weather is on the horizon,
And I know it all too well.
For in my heart, the storms already rage,
While leaving such a bitter tale to tell.
'Cause when the sun was shining,
I knew where it was best to find the shade.
But when dark clouds came rolling in,
So many mistakes were made.
Babe, I watched you leaving slowly,
As if you were the tide.
Castles made of sand erode,
And vanish like my pride.
So my knees they hit the asphalt,
As I begged you not to go.
Yet the empty road left plenty room,
For your tail lights to shine and glow.
And now I'm here with the kind of luck,
That black cats do provide.
For leaving umbrellas open in my mind,
With broken mirrors to coincide.
But please forgive my rambling tongue,
It goes numb without your name to wear.
As the tail lights fade upon my face,
My eyes rain as I'm pretening not to care.
Yet, these internal thunderstorms say otherwise...

FACEDOWN INTERROGATIONS

Do you find me sadistic, darling?
Because in truth, I'm not.
But you already know that.
Since I was actually a masochist around you.
Waiting for you to stop forsaking me.
And maybe even notice the cross I carried for you.
Engraved proudly with your name.
But I've laid that burden down, dear.
Now? I'm in control. Now? I've found a willing victim.
Granted, she doesn't belong to me, either.
But that doesn't make her any less beautiful.
When she's looking up at me,
Or spread open upon the bed.
She isn't afraid like you were.
Her? She intentionally wakes the monster.
She does this knowing
That she will endure the punishment for your crimes.
Your days and hours of neglect.
Her facedown interrogations last for hours.
I fold her body and set it every which way but free.
All because of things that you never did for me.
See? You never came to your senses.
So as her body rains, I make her come instead.
And as her eyes roll into her head, she sees the truth.
And she said to tell you thank you,
For being such a fucking fool.

HOUSE OF CARDS

I am The Suicide King
In this house of cards.
And I knew the foundation was giving way.
But this is what falling for you felt like:
Tumbling down,
Followed by one hard kiss from the ground.
And yet I wonder,
If you ever stop to consider what hurt me worse.
The sudden stop?
Or realizing that I fell alone?

CHERRY BLOSSOM

In my life,
Love has been like a cherry blossom.
Always threatening to show itself.
And soon after it attempts to bloom,
Things begin to die.
Everytime a new goddess wants to peer
behind the walls around my heart,
I eventually let them in.
And then they go running for the hills.
Leaving a life to wither on the vine.
But I never truly die completely.
I always come back.
But that doesn't make it hurt any less.

OH, ICARUS..

Mortality is true in life,
But it doesn't count in love.
It's just another ceiling made of glass,
That we must rise above.
Breaking through is bound to hurt,
Still we do it anyway.
We fear the darkness attached to night,
So we must prolong the day.
And there was a man of equal parts
That was both fool and brave.
But fearlessness was just the whip,
Passion used to tame its' slave.
Oh, Icarus, I'm sick of this
Tell me will it ever end?
I took no joy in warning you,
Since I count you as a friend.
Still you flew too high and got too close,
So it's only right you fell.
But now it's time to take a breath,
And get back on the carousel.
'Cause all of us are seeking warmth,
From our respective sun.
But what on Earth would make you think
That you'd be the lucky one?
To make it past the waiting clouds,
Without paying tax or toll.
But I guess your tunnel vision blurred the line
Between both suicide and goal.
And yet, here he is again,
Proving that fear is what he lacks.
So he will fashion another pair of wings,
That will be held together by some wax.
But Icarus, I'm sick of this
Tell me, will it ever end?
I'll take no joy in mourning you,
Since I count you as my friend.
Still you sought to prove us wrong,

As you accomplished these ungodly feats.
Yet I can't bring myself to be angry with,
A man guided by a heart that beats.

IN THE GARDEN

There is a moment in everyone's life,
When they reach the lover's crossroads.
When you see your lover,
Either bathed in the morning light,
Or lying peaceful, covered in night.
And you think to yourself,
"They are either going to be
The best thing that has ever happened to me...
Or the worst.
I haven't figured it out just yet."
But that's where the beauty in life hides.
Deep in the mystery.
Not knowing what tomorrow will bring.
But aching... truly aching to find out.
Yet here I am. In the garden of the unknown.
Waiting for her...
Not knowing if she will come to me,
As an angel or a serpent.
And being so lonely, that either would do.

IMMUNE

You waited 'til the grass was high,
And then you came.
Without warning, without sound.
Having witnessed my fall here on the uneven ground.
And before I knew it, you were beside me.
By then, it was much too late for resistance to matter.
The fangs were in my veins.
And once it's in your blood,
Your eyes begin to betray you.
For a split second, you think Heaven is in view.
Unaware that your resolve is susceptible to breaking,
During those moments you don't expect.
All the while, the cure for your loneliness is a poison.
But I've become immune to such things.
Rage instead boils my blood,
And quickly distills your efforts.
Then I decapitate you with a written sentence,
And watch as your body flails.
Sure to smile widely as you suffer.

OBLIVIOUS ANGEL

You have no idea what you do to me.
My train of thought has been derailed by your smile,
At least a thousand times.
I stutter, I stammer, and I search
For anything to explain how beautiful you truly are.
While, "good morning, gorgeous"
Is the only thing that manages to escape my lips.
And it is not enough. I want to say more.
But then you emerge from our sea of sheets,
And rush to place your head upon my chest.
As if it were the only thing there to keep you afloat.
There is silence between us,
But for the first time in my life, I am content.
I smile as I feel your fingers interlock with mine.
And I watch, as you listen to my heartbeat
As it echoes like thunder within my chest.
Darling, if it were morse code,
I'm sure that it would proudly spell your name.
But it is with a sadness, that I must now confess
That this will never be my reality.
For you will never belong to me.
Hell, if I'm being honest,
You're an angel that barely knows my name.
Yet, I would give anything to hear you say it,
When you were short of breath.

WEATHERVANES & PAPER PLANES

"It's not that I'm lost, babe.
It's just that I haven't found my way yet,"
She said, with that sparkle in her eyes.
"I don't need weathervanes to point the way.
I go wherever life takes me."
She was so free-spirited, that it made me love her.
She leaned into the wind, with arms outstretched.
Trying to experience weightlessness,
Even if it was only for a single second.
And I can't lie, I was scared.
I was afraid the wind would take her away from me,
Like a paper plane.
Sent right back up to Heaven,
Where the rest of the angels play.
Still, I reached out in hesitation.
As if I was trying to save her from the breeze.
It was then that she looked back and said,
"Before you can get a better grip on life,
You need to learn to let go, baby."
And so, I did.
And that when was when I lost her,
In the light of the sun.

RHYTHM IN THE HAND

I always believed that she was magic,
But she'd pretend it wasn't true.
But certainty arrived inside exposure,
And there was nothing I could do.
For there were pictures set to disappear,
Though I begged them all to stay.
And so she put this rhythm in my hand,
Knowing my wrist would begin to sway.
For this writer has now endured,
The loneliness of the age.
But tonight, her profound enticements,
Won't find their way unto the page.
Because I must hold them in my mind,
If I'm to finish out my task.
I just hope she will cast her spell again,
If it's not too much to ask.
Because she loves to conjure up a storm,
Just before she turns and runs.
And she never sticks around,
To watch as every drop of inspiration comes.

THE LOVER'S CRUCIFIX

Do you have any idea what it takes
To get through the day without you?
I don't think you do, my love.
And yet, it's the night
That always brings the pain of withdrawls.
It's getting much too hard for me to sleep.
And I don't mean difficult, love.
The visions are always the same:
You are lying down, surrendered to me in trust.
And I'm the animal inside of you,
A truth reaffirmed with every thrust.
And while my hand moves with rhythm,
In the dream I lose control.
Trying to bury my love so deep inside of you,
That you will feel it in your soul.
You grasp the sheets with extended hands,
As if you're crucified.
Tonight, there's a rage within my lust,
That will not be denied.
So you wrap your legs around the god,
You've called out to with your breath.
As we sacrifice all your cares,
And introduce your worries to their death.
Darling, you struggle to endure
The depths that I explore.
But the ocean that you do release,
Leaves me exploding like before.

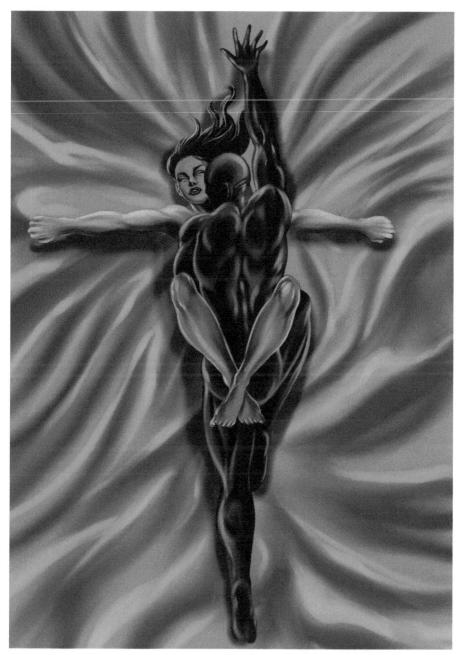

"THE LOVER'S CRUCIFIX" ART BY BOWIE

FOOTPRINTS

All of my life, I have been alone.
Living only within my dreams.
Having been intimate with isolation,
As if I was floating aimlessly in space.
Yet, I have never left the ground.
And so despair became the gravity,
That I could not escape.
But then you came along, baby...
And never in a million years,
Would I think that a woman who looks like you,
Would look at me the way that you do.
Never in a thousand days,
Would I dream that those three words
Could be intended for me,
From lips as intoxicating as yours.
And what you have proven,
In what seems like a hundred, different ways
Is that I was wrong.
And I am delighted to be.
So how can I ever repay you?
Ever since you first kissed me,
I've felt like the reason why
There are footprints on the moon.
And to tell you the truth,
I've yet to come down.

DEATH SENTENCE

Here I am again. In that all too familiar place.
Burning with desire,
And hiding the ashes that smell of desperation.
But in reality, I shouldn't.
For pride is of no use to the kneeling.
Fuck the world and their petty judgments.
Let them know the truth: I ache for you.
I beg for you in my very dreams.
The waves of my lust cause more than tides to rise,
At the merest mention of your name.
I climb the lonely walls of this bell tower,
Hoping you'll return again.
The hands of that goddamn clock...
They bring out the masochist in me.
They might as well be around my neck;
Since I don't want to breathe unless you're near.
Come back, baby.
For the love of everything holy,
Take me back to Heaven with a look.
Make my heart call out for war,
As if it were born in ancient Sparta.
Use your touch,
And help my body rival Pompeii for a day.
Just do anything. Please.
For there are only so many times,
I can call your name,
Before it begins to sound like a death sentence.

RESERVATIONS

Tell me something, darling.
Do I frighten you?
No? Good.
What about my words?
Do they overwhelm you?
No? Good.
Well then, I guess it's the subject matter that makes you
uncomfortable, huh? No?
Well then, what is it?
Why do you only use simple gestures,
To decorate this silence between us?
Is this how you show desire?
Letting my imagination do all the work for you?
Or maybe I just don't do it for you?
If so, that's fine, baby.
Having bad taste is not a capital crime.
It's actually comedy for the gods.
But just remember,
Some will tire of life with reservations.
For lions were meant to run the plains.
And not hold umbrellas in their teeth for you,
Every single time it rains.

RAVENOUS

They don't know what it's like.
They don't see me pacing in the darkness.
They're too busy being content.
They don't know what it's like,
To see such magnificence...
And be overlooked by it.
They have never felt this ache within their bones.
Waiting for a lover that will never come.
To be foaming at the mouth with impatience.
To be starved until ravenous.
And for her?
I am all of the above.
I curse her name a thousand times,
For it is more than my anger that rises.
And she is not here to alleviate this pain.
My medicine walks upright,
And she is too far for me to reach.
I'm going crazy in this cage.
And imagination no longer holds the key.
Only the real thing will suffice!
Or else this world must be forced,
To pay the eternal price.

THE FABRIC OF MY SOUL

Darling, forgive me if I'm a nuisance
Or even needy in the least.
For it was in the fabric of my soul,
That loneliness had left a crease.
And it's when I tried to smooth it out,
That the edges start to roll.
So insecurity jumps behind the wheel,
To often steer and take control.
That's when panic starts setting in,
And I feel you slip away.
So I go into overdrive,
And start begging you to stay.
I know that reassurance is growing old,
But I swear that this isn't my intent.
It's just losing the greatest thing I have ever known,
That I am trying to prevent.
Especially since my memories are collecting dust,
And I hear them beg for company.
So I suggest we reunite,
While hoping you won't run from me.
For what's the use of my salvation,
If I can no longer feel its' grace?
I find the only times that I am whole,
Are when I feel your hands upon my face.
So if I beg you to rescue me,
Know that it's not for lack of pride.
I'm just overwhelmed by love, and don't want to be denied.
Won't you save me slowly, baby?

WHEN THE SUN FINALLY SETS

I never thought there would be a day,
That I would gladly write or say.
That I can see myself with you,
When we're both old and gray.
We'll be sitting on our porch,
Watching grandchildren in the yard.
Oh, I can see it crystal clear
My dear, it isn't very hard.
All I do is close my eyes,
And I can watch it fall in place.
For every day feels like a gift,
When I'm beside you in this space.
And to see you still flash a smile,
Despite the lines upon my face.
Proves there is no expiration date
On your love, my saving grace.
And though there will come a day,
When we succumb to time.
You will live forever, love
And be kept eternal in my rhyme.
For you will be the Queen,
That your King will forever hail.
And when the sun finally sets on life,
I'll find you again beyond the veil.

THE FERRYMAN'S TOLL

How on Earth can I express, the way I truly feel?
To the one who touched my wounds,
And helped them start to heal.
For I've bled for many years,
And some never saw a drop.
So there were no tourniquets,
To help the bleeding stop.
But she came up to me,
With arms she did extend.
And despite my disbelief,
I have indeed begun to mend.
See? The hunger of my doubts,
Fed on my lack of self-respect.
But when you're alone for so many years,
What else could you expect?
Yet she is now helping me to see,
These doubts are only lies.
And she took away my fears,
Then placed these pennies upon their eyes.
Signifying that she is aware,
There's a toll on the river Styx.
For she was willing to pay the cost,
On behalf of this broken man she fixed.
And since the ferryman is paid, I feel I must rejoice.
While I sing her praise, until I strain my voice.
'Cause I once swore that I was cursed,
And I still feel that I was right.
But as long as she is alive, how can I deny the light?

A WISH IN WINTER

It was at the end of a long, winter day
That his hard work would be rewarded.
Fighting traffic,
He rushed home as if his life depended on it.
And after what seemed to be an endless struggle,
Finally, he arrived;
His seemingly eternal wait had reached its end.
He opened the front door,
Eagerly wanting to see the only thing that mattered:
And it was her.
But alas, this time, she wasn't waiting by the door.
He took a few, puzzled steps into the house,
And there she was...
Fast asleep on their humble couch.
Looking like an angel exhausted from flight.
He walked over and knelt beside his dreaming Queen.
And for a few moments, he marveled at her.
How did he ever get so lucky?
Knowing in his very soul,
That she was the answer to a wish
That never left his lips.
He gently raised his rough and worn hand,
Moved her hair out of her face,
And gently kissed her forehead.
Then he very softly placed his jacket over her,
And disappeared into the rest of the house.
For he knew, that all was right in the world.

UNAPOLOGETIC GODS

I'm much too reserved in person.
So despite my stature, you may not notice me.
But in my mind? That kingdom behind my eyes?
You have been mine, at least a thousand times.
I have left this chair,
Like Zeus descending from Olympus;
And pinned you to the nearest wall as if you were fine art.
I have held handfuls of your hair;
The way that Poseidon holds his trident,
And ravaged you from behind.
I have lain you beneath me,
And pounded your shores like the tide.
Darling, I am gentle when you crave it.
But I am merciless, when you have misbehaved.
And no one knows the lengths I'd go,
To give you every inch of mine.
In my mind, we divide and conquer
Like unapologetic gods.
And oh, if you only knew
What I dreamed of doing to you,
During those times that your beauty leaves me silent...

ALCHEMY

Today, much like centuries past,
This practice is forbidden.
Often derided by the uninitiated as immoral,
And decried by the pious as the devil's work.
But all of them were wrong.
The spark is all that matters.
Transmutation breathes the air of divinity.
All other perspectives fall prey to semantics.
She was the only element I needed.
For it was at the very base of my being,
That I was broken.
Through her touch, I became whole.
In time, one could even say noble.
Her love made the impossible seem effortless.
Like turning lead into gold.
One look from her, and inside I am alive.
One kiss from her, and inside I am ablaze.
And at the first moment, I am inside of her,
I am a god.
Through our union there is alchemy.
Nothing else makes life worth living.

DEVOUR

Sometimes,
No matter how hard you try
You just can't get your mind out of the gutter.
And honestly, when it comes to you,
I don't really want to, baby.
I want to keep you there
With make-up smeared, and dirty knees
Looking up at me.
Waiting for me to come down there,
And devour you...

DANGEROUS GAME

Darling, we are playing a dangerous game.
Ignoring those who may have brought us to the dance,
We are recklessly lost in each other.
Along the razor's edge we glide,
Without a care in the world.
Guilt will not cut in to steal you from me tonight.
I will have you at all costs.
Consequences needn't come,
If discretion is our guide.
But we both know,
Secrets tend not to hide very well from fate.
Yet one thing still echoes in my mind,
Why does this dance feel better than all the others?

BLOOD FROM THE STONES

She was the type of woman,
Who made a man wonder if he was to be
Another notch on her bedpost;
Or maybe even a new head for her mantle.
But what she failed to realize
Is that this life is a thresher.
And for a night free of banality,
Some lambs walk proudly into slaughter.
For not every man is able to walk on water,
Before they die and return to live again.
No, there are some who'd rather be ridden hard
And put away broken-hearted;
Than to spend their days alone,
Until they finally died within.
So do not spare us from your claws, darling.
Draw blood from the stones, if that is your will.
For I have died inside long enough,
And I would rather it be time that you killed.

SECRETS BLOOM IN GRAVES

Tell me something, darling.
And it will stay just between us.
What is the thing that your body craves?
What is the thought that never leaves you alone,
And always keeps you warm
Down in the most sacred of places?
Will you share it with me?
And take advantage of my knack for keeping secrets?
Knowing that I will take so many things to the grave?
Do you need to make that confession, baby?
Feel free to do so. For you are always safe with me.
Whether you are ready to instruct or to be punished,
I am ready to grant your wish.
I just need to know if you're brave enough,
To pay the purest pleasure's price.
See, I'm not asking for forever, baby.
No, with what I have in mind...
A few hours will suffice.

THE MONSTERS WE BECAME

I won't engage your understanding,
I won't engage your pride.
I'd rather ignore all the foolish things,
You chose to hold inside.
I'd rather engage your silence,
Since it's what you've shown me best.
So please suppress that pathetic thing,
Making noise within your chest.
For it once longed to call for mine,
And now I'd rather not respond.
So place your hand across its mouth,
Until it chokes on memories considered fond.
For my patience has expired,
And my resolve bears a jagged edge.
So I have no desire to join the dance,
You've long since started on the ledge.
Oh, so many get their thrills
From playing people like a game.
Then they cower in the corners,
From these monsters we became.
So go on and play the victim,
Tell them how I came baring claws and teeth.
And just leave out the part about the loneliness,
You've left me buried still beneath.

PRICELESS EXCHANGE

If these words were currency,
Could I buy your attention for awhile?
Maybe move my wrist once or twice,
Just to earn that gorgeous smile.
Could these paragraphs inspire laughs?
Maybe even a game of truth or dare?
Leaving proof of confessions made,
As we did things far beyond compare.
For I long to be included in your future,
And I wish to understand your past.
But I'll also ensure this present moment,
Will find a way to last.
'Cause I feel it is my duty,
To secure a place to rest your head.
As my hands move across your body,
To reveal the things I've never said.
And as I taste the inspiration,
That by now is sure to flow.
I will cherish your expression,
As you discover just how deep this quill can go.

HOWLS OF THE HUNGRY

These words are the howls of a hungry wolf,
Calling to the moons within your eyes.
Pacing in the wilderness,
Hoping to escape the blackness in the skies.
So won't you come around again,
And shine your light my way?
Or must I hunt you down and seek you out,
To turn the willing into prey.

WEIGHTLESS

They say that fall season is upon us;
But me, I merely call it autumn.
Because I fell for you over a year ago.
And though life has found a way
To eclipse me from your view,
You still shine like the moon in my memories.
Pulling me and pushing me away,
Just like I was the tide.
They don't know that your gravity is inescapable, my love.
And every time you looked at me,
I would just fall further for you;
Exactly like those suicidal leaves.
I know nothing will catch me these days
Except for the ground;
And yet, I just can't help myself.
Only your love, your touch, your kiss
Can make a man this heavy,
Feel like he's weightless.

AFTER-MARKET LOVE

Well, darling...
I've made a few attempts at transference, now.
But all of them end the same way:
Right back at square one.
The latest claims she wanted me inside of her.
But when it came time to come,
Something else always came up for her.
And that's fine. I was only fooling myself anyways.
How could I ever substitute your prescription strength
For her after-market love?
What would take her hands time to do to me,
You could accomplish with just a look.
Sure, she inspired growth in parts of a lonely man;
But only you kept the reactor in the red, baby.
And I know you feel it too.
Though on some nights, you settle for just enough.
But I know he doesn't get as deep as I do.
I know he doesn't inspire awe,
When you hold him in your hands.
Not everyone brings out the fiend in you, baby.
When you're ready to hurt inside again,
You will remember my name.
'Cause I haven't forgotten yours.
And I know damn well, these side effects...
They make slaves out of all of us.

YOUR GHOST

I can't pretend I haven't changed since you went away.
It would be a lie to say otherwise.
But here I am; knee deep in my routine.
Acting as if your departure was nothing but a dream.
Yet the truth is, your ghost haunts me
Everywhere I go in this town.
Every sight is a slap in the face;
Cruel reminders that you are not around.
Every stop, every turn
Was another lesson that I refused to learn.
These red lights often mock me,
When I wonder if you have missed me so.
And the green lights recall the night,
When you wished I didn't have to go.
Do you remember it?
That night when you were the envy of the moon,
And we swore that fireflies danced for us.
I'm sure that you don't.
Those kinds of things are best swept beneath the rug.
Where no one else can see.
And even after all of this time, I hope you found a way
To make your life better than the way it used to be.
For I cannot say the same.

DARKNESS COMES

I often lie awake at night;
Staring at the ceiling, as if it contained wonders.
But given enough time,
My mind always finds its way to you.
And it's then I wonder, what you are doing.
Knowing you, you are helping someone else.
Doing so with the heart and grace I have come to love.
I wonder if you know about the space next to me,
That's waiting to hold you, almost as much as I am.
I know I am a fool for chasing down these thoughts.
But they are my only source of light,
Every time the darkness comes.
And each time it visits, I fear that it's here to stay.
That is why sometimes I beg you
To say those three words;
For it is your voice, and your voice alone...
That makes my demons go away.

HOWL AT THE MOON

My lips have caressed your name a thousand times.
Each having tasted better than the last.
And on these lonely nights,
I salivate at the very thought of you.
Baby, you must know by now what you do to me.
I'm here in the darkness, pacing back and forth.
Counting the times you've failed to look my way.
Knowing full well, that you'll pay for every one of
them, the next time that I'm inside of you.
The wolf within takes umbrage with being ignored.
And when I see you glowing in the distance,
I have no choice but to seethe.
For every day without you,
Is a day that I don't want to breathe.
But you make me do just that.
And so, I'm here doubled over in hunger pains.
Since you always leave me Famished.
Now I must put pen to paper in your honor,
Hoping you'll hear my written howls at the moon.

UNHEARD SCREAMING

I've told you how I felt so many times,
My voice has gone hoarse.
Overexertion has caused those once proud expressions of
passion, to have been distilled down into whispers.
But let us be honest, love...
You weren't listening,
Even when there was still thunder in my words.
You have supplied me with a cavalcade of excuses
That you've masterfully shaped throughout the years.
And in those moments of your defiance,
The only person you convinced was yourself.
For I will never believe that you are unworthy of the tides
of my love, that I've wished to submerge you within.
And I will never concede that there could be a better man
Who will provide, protect, and spend his nights on side of
you; and when you wished it, inside of you.
I am that one, darling.
The anomaly.
The exception to the rules
You've been so busy carving in stone, that you couldn't
hear me as I was screaming your name.

FOG

She knows my combination well.
A few twists and turns, and my inhibitions dissipate.
And I begin to come undone.
She has a subtle way of lighting this spark.
Two prolonged kisses,
She stops midway through the third;
Then she just looks at me.
And I feel like the luckiest man alive.
Next she flashes a sly and subtle smile,
Before she leans in to finish what she started.
And just like that... I am gone.
I never know where I go.
But it's goodbye, Dr. Jekyll; and hello Mr. Clyde.
And I go from humble king
To raging beast in her hands.
I tear into her like I haven't eaten in years.
The arch in her back is the envy of the crescent moon
that draws the tides so effortlessly.
And I watch the oceans in her eyes widen, as I enter
her temple with reckless abandon.
I engage in the ancient art of demolition,
Until the fog in my mind clears.
And finally, as we are adrift in the seas of our own
creation, I remember exactly who I am.
And I know that I will never love another soul as
much or the way that I love her.

COME ALIVE

I've seen you from afar,
And dreamed you were close enough to taste.
So now I often spend my days,
Wishing the night would come with haste.
'Cause it's when I close my eyes,
I can pretend that you are mine.
And I'm free to live a dream with you,
Far from the vengeful hands of time.
Darling, I lie as still I can be,
Just to keep you here with me.
For Hell comes with the morning sun,
Leaving my time in Heaven done.
And I've nothing here to offer you,
Except both a tattered heart and pride.
But if you came home to me,
I swear you could watch me come alive.
Imagine all the lonely nights,
Without you in my bed.
Imagine all the judgmental things,
That have echoed in my head.
And try to picture everything,
You could save with all your love.
I've prayed for this so many times,
But I fear there is no one listening up above.

SAFE HARBOR

In this year plus of ours, I made her many promises.
Many of them will be known to no one but us;
But you should know I've done my best to keep them all.
I remember telling her that she was safe now.
That she had nothing to worry about.
Because no matter what life threw at us,
We would face it together.
Because I knew the waters of her past were turbulent.
And yet I told her, despite the darkness of my depression,
my heart and soul would always be her lighthouse.
That these open arms would never be her prison;
But rather, they would be her safe harbor.
So when she tired of swimming,
She could capsize between them,
And I would hold her until the morning.
No thanks would ever be needed.
Because that is what you do
When you love someone more than you love yourself:
You protect them.
And as I lie alone in this bed,
Even after all of this time...
I wonder if I still shine brightly enough
For her to find her way back home.

MURDER ME

You left me twisting in the wind,
For what has felt like years.
Now you sing your saddest song,
And expect my eyes to bring you tears.
But dear, it seems the well is dry,
And my heart no longer beats.
Since you left me as a chalk outline,
On these unforgiving streets.
You say you cannot find a soul,
Who will finally treat you right.
And yet, you overlooked the one
Who always reminded you to fight.
Because a coward's what you are,
You'll face anything but love.
And it's your disposition that,
You're unwilling to rise above.
But in the next life that we lead,
I'm sure you'll continue hurting me.
I just wish you'd finally grow a pair,
So you could murder me with certainty.

STARVATION

When it comes to love, the only thing more
damaging than time is distance.
On lonely nights, it feels like distance is a tumor
that grows violently inside of love.
Eating me alive from the inside out.
But then, relief arrives.
All I have to do is see you, or speak to you,
And I am once again flooded with desire.
Instantly, I'm reminded why
I endure the torture of waiting for you.
Cravings have written your name across my bones.
Only your hands can quell the lust that rages within
these impatient limbs.
Only your lips can quiet the demons whispering in
these over-receptive ears, love.
And only your body feels like home, when you
willingly anoint and allow me inside.
Won't you return, darling?
Just one kiss, and it's like you never left.
I can almost exhale the smoke, that you get me high
enough to breathe. So speak to me, love.
Tell me that you still ache for me, in the places that
you can't reach. And I'll be beside you in a dream,
until I can ravage you for real.
I'm waiting impatiently, baby.
And I'm dying of starvation.

WHEN THE MONSTER WAKES

Darling, you don't understand.
Hell, I don't think you ever have.
Seeing you in person always does something to me.
It's hard to put into words;
But not nearly as hard as you make me with just a look.
And you know it, don't you?
I see you bite your lip, and it's then the change begins.
Deep behind my eyes,
I hear chains reach their breaking points.
And to me, that can only mean one thing:
You have awakened the monster.
I hear it as it runs toward you;
Impatient breaths merging with joyous howls.
Then in a flash, you are lifted off the ground;
And pressed against the nearest wall.
My teeth are quickly buried in your neck,
As even the picture frames tremble from my power.
Tonight, the only god's mercy you will pray for is mine.
And you will be ravaged until the sun comes pouring
into our humble home.
For you must learn the consequences
Of making me wait as long you have;
Knowing that you are everything that I need.
Since the starving cannot be controlled,
Once they begin to feed.

LA DANSE DANS LA VALLÉE

Her legs went up into the air like mountains;
As her elbows held her up, in a position just the same.
It has been a long time, since she's felt this alive.
The days bore down upon her with such a weight,
That even the nights brought her pain.
But right now, in this second, she was free.
As she collapsed backward onto the bed,
Her hands found their way into my hair;
As if to hold me in place as I drank from her chalice.
The legs that once made Kilimanjaro blush,
Now fashion themselves into a vice around my neck.
She feels so much closer to transcendence now;
And so I press forward with zeal.
I continue speaking in silent tongues,
The language that only she can understand.
And as her body quakes,
I know for a moment that her pain is gone.
So I proudly continue, allowing each lash of this tongue,
To course through her body like lightning.
And each time she trembles,
I can't help but to gaze upon my works.
I feel divine, as I hear my name decorate each space
between her breaths.
For I am honored to be her medicine.

CLOCKWISE

I wonder if I bought you flowers,
Would you just sit and let them wilt?
What if I impaled you with my love,
Would you take it right up to the hilt?
Or would you point to circumstance
And lay the blame upon its feet?
Could I gently slide my fingers in,
And turn your bitter into sweet?
Tell me all the things that trouble you
As my hand goes clockwise for a time.
Lose yourself inside my words,
And bathe your subconscious in my rhyme.
Bring forth the ocean springs,
That could cleanse your worried heart.
For I wish to see you come undone,
And I don't mean to fall apart.

THE UNSPOKEN POWER

Her lips were as soft as an angel's wings.
And she surely tasted like God's saving grace.
On her tongue lied resurrection's bliss.
While Heaven surely looked like her smiling face.
And I was eternally grateful that she smiled often.
Because she knew that it was the power of her kiss,
That made me her Lazarus.

SET IN STONE

So many people grow frustrated with me...
I can feel it.
Because the way I see myself,
Is not the way they do when using their own eyes.
They feel as though their words ring hollow in my ears.
As if I'm listening, and yet, still fail to hear them.
But I hear everything;
It's just that words no longer hold any weight with me.
Which, I'll be honest, is disheartening;
Given that it is written words that pour so profusely from
my heart and from my soul.
They tell me all the time that I deserve better;
But so very few ever show me.
Sure, some encourage and some flirt;
But in the end, it is only the silence that looms.
And so I turn inward;
Using memories of her to keep me warm.
For the thought of her is filled with more love, that the
reality of my darkened days.
So hear me when I say, that this is not a phase.
I sit. I wait. And I will only move for her;
As if I was truly set in stone.
Because she once made the effort, to call me her own.
So who am I to deny her of my love?

INSCRIBED IN BRAILLE

We find ourselves in trying times,
Each with our cross to bear.
But when it's you upon my mind
Darling, I don't have another care.
I drift away through memories,
And get drunk off your perfume.
The recollections dance so vividly,
I wake and look for you inside the room.
It kills me now to see you there,
As true love is denied to you.
'Cause you know the only times I've felt alive,
Are when I was inside of you.
And I know that what you settle for does not compare
To the depths I often reached.
You never had to say a word,
I learned the lessons your body had to teach.
I know your every subtle move,
And I heard demands you never spoke.
I tried to penetrate your heart and soul,
Until my love had made you choke.
Still no one else has ever done,
The things you've done to me.
And if other women saw the beast you helped create,
They would surely run from me.
But only you could take what I had to give,
And survive to tell the tale.
For we still proudly bear each other's mark,
As if it were inscribed in Braille.

ONE THROUGH FIVE

Loving you was the worst thing I've ever done.
Promises meant nothing to you:
And neither did I.
I gave you everything,
And kept nothing for myself.
You proved that words mean nothing.
Written or spoken.
Through these words, you were once worshiped.
Never again.

SIX THROUGH TEN

He's with you, I breathed you. There's a difference.
Only the loved can kill the living with silence.
You never understood the depths I felt for you.
I once thought I had forever to earn you.
Now I see that you already saw past me.

END OF ACT I

"I think anyone who opened their heart enough to love without restraint and subsequently were devastated by loss knows that in that moment you are forever changed; a part of you is no longer whole. Some will never again love with that level of abandon where life is perceived as innocent and the threat of loss seems implausible. Love and loss, therefore, are linked."

- Donna Lynn Hope

"Ever has it been that love knows not its own depth until the hour of separation."

- *Kahlil Gibran*

2
OBSERVATIONS

"We pass through the present with our eyes blindfolded. We are permitted merely to sense and guess at what we are actually experiencing. Only later when the cloth is untied can we glance at the past and find out what we've experienced and what meaning it has."

- Milan Kundera

THE HERMIT

WEIGHED AND WANTING

I want to write, but I can't.
I feel the words flow until they stop.
Like there is a dam inside my mind.
And the doubts are piled skyward like logs.
Jamming the flow of what once was mighty.
But like water, they seep out...
Little by little, almost letter by letter.
They flow; and slowly form words.
But only further downstream.
Yet when all is said and done, it doesn't matter.
This is the way of the world.
Nature has its ebbs and flows.
Its comes and goes.
The true purpose for anything, nobody really knows.
But we are all seeking our balance.
Our environmental equilibrium.
We hope that our material purchases,
Or our antiquated faiths,
Will provide us with sufficient counterweights.
And balance the scales of life.
But not me.

MEASURED IN GRAMS

Exhaustion dulls the mind.
Causing the senses to grind to a halt.
The only thing that remains, is the anger.
It hides well behind the eyes,
Like an ocean of acid.
In which, I want to drown the dreams of others.
But for now, cutting will suffice.
So I cut all of my ties to them.
And watch them float farther away from me.
Like a child's lost balloon,
Or a kite that has lost its appeal.
I let it drift and drift away.
Hoping the sun will reduce them to ashes,
Causing them to fall back to the Earth.
Worthless and humbled.
The same way my sun once caused me to fall.
But there's no safety net for stupidity.
And there's no hope for reconciliation.
Hope is just a drug for remedial junkies.
Useless; and unworthy of its weight in grams.

BOUNDS OF GRAVITY

Disappointment...
Does your gravity know no bounds?
For I have tried and tried to escape your grasp,
But you are too strong, friend.
And while your bitter embrace has grown tighter
over the years,
Please don't mistake my reluctant acceptance
As some form of subtle gratitude.
For I'd rather be alone,
Than to spend more time getting to know you.
But maybe you've listened...
Because when I look around,
I realize that I am the tree in the forest.
And I haven't made a sound.

BALL POINT WRISTS

Writing is my salvation.
It is a debt that must be paid in ink.
So now the page has become the cross,
On which I'll sacrifice, all the delightful things I think.
And I must sharpen my mind into a blade,
In the hopes of getting these ball point wrists to bleed.
Then I'll be submerged in pools of black,
Until I reach the catharsis that I need.
But such a thing cannot be rushed,
No, the words will flow in time.
And most won't be satisfied,
Until they're coaxed to rhyme.
For they know inspiration is a fleeting mistress,
Who is not promised to return.
And when she arrives to ignite your fires,
Then the pages must be burned.

OH, THE HUMANITY...

We are the living dead.
Contrite, soulless consumers.
Watching dreams asphyxiate on the vines,
Before they blossom into the lives we want to lead.
Our minds are watered down
With high-definition projections;
From the flashing screens
That illuminate our rooms like gods.
And we wait.
Like fools, we wait for happiness
To go on its Black Friday sale.
And since there are no coupons for success,
We look to satellites, to steer us to the nearest shortcut.
For we'd rather spin the wheel, and make a deal
Than to bide our time, and earn our meal.
My, what fools we are...
Blind to the ends of our nose.
Junkies for the names in our pockets and on our clothes.
Self-worth measured in likes and shares.
Coming from the same, anonymous zealots,
Throwing stones from digital glass homes.
Hoping to avoid their victim's angry stares.
Knowing we'll be judged by the jury of our peers.
Forgetting that dying before we really live,
Should be the greatest of our fears.
But in the end, what do I know? I'm only human after all.

UNDERTOW

One can have their eyes wide open,
And still not be awake.
Just as one can have their eyes tightly shut,
And not even be asleep.
And like this bit of irony,
My stoic disposition can be deceiving at times.
I'm slowly learning,
That there is far more to me than anger.
I've become aware that having less baggage,
Makes for truly lighter travels.
And I've noticed that my actions are better received,
If I play only to a crowd of one.
But that's not the way life pans out for us.
We must roll with the waves,
As if they were punches.
Otherwise, we'll be swept off our feet,
Time and time again.
And believe me,
Toxic opinions are far easier to escape,
Than the unseen pull of the undertow.

DIFFERENCES

The difference between men and boys,
Is the realization
Of the importance of women.
And the difference between women and girls,
Is the realization
That they don't need the validation of other women,
Much less that of men.

EXPRESSIONS OF CHANGE

Words are given life by expression.
But beliefs are given life by practice.
And I believe that with enough practice,
A man can change.
He cannot always change the world,
But he can change his place within it.
And that is why I believe
That the measure of a man
Is not the speed with which he accepts credit or praise.
But rather, the speed with which
He is willing to shoulder blame.
For how can he correct the wrongs of the world,
If he cannot first correct his own?

OBSTRUCTIONS

Very few people
Ever truly acknowledge their flaws.
Yet those of us who can,
Often have trouble looking past them.

WITH HEAVY HEARTS

If our hearts were meant to bleed
Then at times, why are they so heavy?
It is because we place upon them
The burdens of the mind
And the sorrows of the soul.
So, in this world
Where we are destined to float away
Into selfishness and decadence...
Our hearts are so heavy,
Because they are our anchors.

THE POWER OF CHOICE

Circumstances may help to shape a man
But his choices are what make him.
So if you ever see a man
Whose ways are set in stone...
Know then that you have seen a man
Who is at the end of his rope.

SPEAK WITH CARE

Speaking with certainty,
Inspires a confidence that breathes the air of arrogance.
Speaking with belief,
Inspires a knowledge that allows room for errors.
And speaking with doubt,
Invites a quest to seek and ascertain conviction.
But I, my friend, am certain
That I will never have all the answers.
And I believe
That I was never meant to have all of the answers.
And I doubt
That many of you will disagree.

ABLE AND WILLING?

Unless you are willing to accept
ONLY what you truly deserve,
Then you truly deserve,
Only what you are willing to accept.

THE DANGER WITH BELIEFS

There is nothing more dangerous
Than a man who believes what he says.
Especially, when the things he says,
Sound like they are beyond belief.
Yet it has been said,
That power is gained through persuasion,
And not brute force.
But having said all of that,
It is through the strength of my words
That I am merely a few sentences away
From creating an army.
So tell me...
Does that make me dangerous?

CIVILIZATIONS

It is not the man who can move mountains
That should be feared.
For his power lies solely in the body.
And over time, the body will break down.
If it is not already made to break by others.
Who should be feared then?
Well, I'll tell you...
It is the man who believes he can move mountains,
That should be feared.
For his power lies in faith.
And faith has moved more than mountains.
It has moved civilizations.
Both closer together, and farther apart.

REVERENCE

The accomplishments of the living
Will be tarnished by judgment.
It is only in death,
That legends receive their reverence.
So while many of us
Will be hated while we are here.
We can rest assured knowing
That they will love us when we are gone.

THE BUSY LIVES OF GODS

Having just sat down, I told myself to write.
But in truth, I don't have much to say.
Local sports teams are busy,
Receving sound defeats.
Mother Nature is seemingly growing more displeased.
News updates are breaking,
And are even more disheartening.
Can anybody tell me what's going on?
Where on Earth is the love?
Don't bother telling me about the prophets
Or their prophecies espoused for profit.
Don't bother telling me to hit my knees
While begging for some divine miracle.
And don't bother asking me,
What we should do about all of this.
Because I don't know.
All I do know,
Is that we need love and understanding
Now more than ever.
And if people are praying for peace,
Then their gods must be deaf.
Or just plain busy.

PUSHPINS & YARN

I will never understand people.
And no amount of reading or analyzing will help me.
Patterns of behavior,
Are just part of a larger tapestry.
Like the ones on those crime shows.
People are on the bulletin board...
Their lives connected by pushpins & yarn.
Their actions are seemingly devoid of logic.
Their compassion being smothered
Beneath the weight of inflating prides.
Even when so much can be learned in silence.
So much can be missed,
When there is dischord in a bustling room.
Senses dull and details blur.
And we are left to wonder why in the aftermath.
Has all of the hot air that we've blown,
Caused the red flags to wave where we couldn't see?
Have the answers been just below our noses?
Just obscured from our lines of sight?
Or is it that we're just looking in the wrong places?
Too busy looking up, instead of ahead.
Too busy looking back,
When that's not the perspective that we lack.
I guess it's too hard for us to see anything,
Past the shadows of our own ideals.

MODERN PARADOX

My, how insatiable we are.
As children, we simply cannot wait to get older.
To live seemingly free of restrictions;
And bask in the utter freedoms of adulthood.
But then, as adults,
We find ourselves looking in the rearview mirror.
Wishing we were young again.
Allowed to have room for errors.
No matter how grand or grave.
To be unencumbered by responsibility,
And unaware of the opinions of others.
True freedom.
How insane is that?
We always see true freedom as unattainable.
We never realize that we've had it,
Until we become slaves to something else.
It is the paradox of our times.
Will we ever learn,
To squeeze the juices from today?
For there are no second tries,
Once the wellspring has run dry.
We must live with hunger;
And drink our passions until we're drowned.
Or else, we'll be buried by regrets.

YELLING AT A WHISPER

Do you hear that sound?
No? How could you?
It's so loud in here,
You can barely hear yourself think...
But the sound I am referring to is me.
Here. Now. Screaming at the top of my lungs.
But in a place this crowded,
You'll never hear me, though.
So I may as well be yelling at a whisper.
Everybody's shuffling past me.
At break-neck speeds, tempered with knee-jerk reactions.
Everyone is so busy,
So enamored with their hand-held screens,
That they don't have time to picture my thoughts,
Or even download my dreams.
It's a struggle.
Because, truly, I don't write for recognition,
Nor do I type to see my name in lights.
I do this to preserve my own sanity.
I do this because drugs, alcohol, and /or therapy
Can become expensive habits.
Writing costs me nothing; yet, remains a priceless vice.
And strangely, through this venture,
It is I who ends up being free.
Even if no one notices.

HEELING WOUNDS

Look at us. So proud, so boastful.
Sharing and tweeting our short soliloquies.
Whilst feeling so self-righteous,
That we actually think the world should stop turning,
And take note.
But like in so many other things,
The disappointment finds us.
No matter how deeply we hide within ourselves,
There is no escape.
It smells our fear, and burrows behind our eyes
Until it reaches our minds.
Raising every alarm within reach.
Our expectations betray us, you see?
They leave a trail of crumbs across our senses;
Allowing disappointment to creep unencumbered,
And slip behind our best defenses.
I guess we must be humbled.
Because in truth, so many of us have lived
Beneath the bootheel of fate,
That we've forgotten how to stand up straight.
And you wanna know something crazy?
I don't even see the footprints on my back anymore.

HAMSTER WHEEL

Friend, the sands are falling down.
In truth, they always do.
I don't think they have ever stopped.
Only our perception of them changes.
And they have never been good or evil.
They just are.
Granted, they will always exert some control over us;
But that doesn't make them tyrants.
Nor conquerors in the least.
That's just the martyr in all of us talking.
We all just want our moment in the sun.
To feel the eyes of the world upon us.
Even if we have to be on a cross to get them.
That's the price we will gladly pay to play.
For this is just a big game after all.
The Unseen play it on a cosmic level.
The powerful move their pieces behind closed doors.
While the rest of us, try our collective bests,
Just to make it through the goddamn day.
Because if we're lucky enough to see tomorow,
The Unseen will turn the hourglass over;
And it will all begin anew.
Time is a flat circle, I was told.
I guess it's up to us then, to make it feel less and less,
Like a giant, hamster wheel.

STRAITJACKETS

What is there left to say?
You wear your disinterest like a Scarlet Letter.
And I have to restrain my anger just to talk to you.
Excuses fall from your lips,
Like leaves still reeling from Autumn's kiss.
But don't insult my fucking intelligence, dear.
People go after what they want in their hearts.
They don't run back to the slaughterhouse,
Just because the butcher calls.
God... How foolish can we be?
You're expecting change,
And I'm holding onto hope.
Both of us ignoring the truth:
When it comes to matters of the heart,
History will always outweigh possibility.
Proving that comfort zones,
Are merely straitjackets for the sane.

ADORNED

Everyone wants to be the martyr in their own story.
Whether they feel the cross is literal or metaphoric,
That matters not.
They still wish to be cast, as the selfless hero.
Besieged by their enemies on all sides.
But often, they leave out the most pertinent of details.
Conveniently, they fail to mention their own crimes.
So eager to be adorned with their crown of thorns,
They forget the bones finding homes,
Within their collective closets.

IMPRESSION

I lie alone in the darkness.
Some would probably call this depression.
But I am at peace.
Thoughts race to flood the corners with anxiety;
But eventually, they subside.
And I am at peace.
See? There are no expectations in the blackness.
Insecurities have to stumble about blindly,
But they never find anywhere to rest comfortably.
And so, for the moment, I am at peace.
Although this bed knows no impression but my own,
Things are as they should be.
Neither dreams nor make believe,
Bring any comfort to me.
And so I rest my weary frame,
And try to convince myself...
That I am at peace.

SELF-RIGHTEOUS MATHEMATICS

Are you happy now, my dear?
Do your crossed arms bring a smile?
Have you come down from your highest horse,
To now begin the trial?
Have you sentenced me for crimes,
That I've committed in my mind?
All while overlooking facts,
And ignoring the evidence you find?
Since you're so quick to pass judgment
When things don't go your way.
Then you impose restrictions on your life
Thinking it's best to keep temptations well at bay.
Well darling, that may work for you,
But for me it's worth a laugh.
For a righteous one is still alone,
When there is no else to do the math.
So just know that I will not apologize,
And I'll let my pride come before the fall.
For I refuse to ever deny desires,
That only make me human after all.

SMOKE SIGNALS

There is a profound difference
In writing because you have something to say
And saying something because you wished to write.
Because while the latter may turn out to be alright,
It will always be the former that will truly matter.
Me? I need the words to sear inside my mind,
Before I will allow them to brand my tongue.
My heart is a raging furnace,
And I wish you all to read my signals in the smoke.
There is too much misplaced passion in this world.
And there is far too much blood boiling,
And not enough pulsing through our better parts.
For I'd much rather write
Of longing for her to come,
Than to keep wishing that Armageddon would.
When will we ever tire,
Of repeating our many historical mistakes?
When will enough ever truly be enough?
Or will the coins thrown in the well,
Continue paying for our empty promises?

ECHOES UNHEARD

Serenades echo in the distance.
Do you hear them?
Do they come roaring like the tide,
Or whispering like the wind?
Has the crescendo met your expectations?
Or is your front row seat much too close for comfort?
Tell me. Won't you, please?
I'm trying to understand your dilemma, darling.
Symphonies will often overwhelm,
Those who have been conditioned by noise.
Oh, how I ache for you.
Knowing that so many admire your rose from afar,
But will never brave your thorns with open arms.
Yet here I am,
Digging up memories to fill the void.
My, what fools we are!
Each of us playing songs for the other,
And yet we keep performing for those who won't listen.

PENNY FOR YOUR THOUGHTS

Is this another instance,
Where my observations have been made?
And placed like coins inside a jar,
To prove that attention has been paid?
Now do you need assurance?
Maybe a receipt that verifies?
That every single thing you do,
Plays out before my eyes.
Girl, is there another lesson
That I'm now supposed to learn?
Like something profound about the tables,
And how they're prone to turn?
But please spare me the quotations,
And clichés you've overused.
Just give me something truthful,
Or are you still broken and confused?
Because now I hear that your behavior
Is wearing thin to say the least.
Which suggests to me your actions
May have left your self-respect deceased.

BARBARIANS & KINGS

My better nature is a weakness,
That I've done my best to exorcise.
So many compliment my disposition,
Yet fail to look me in the eyes.
Hiding truth inside of pleasantries,
They claim they fail to understand.
How this laundry list of qualities
Could reside within just a single man.
But it's easier to comprehend,
If you read between the lines.
For I've countered all their arguments,
At least a thousand times.
While some will chalk it up to chance,
And others a lack of confidence
They always overlook the obvious,
'Cause they can escape the consequence.
But such an egregious oversight,
Often boils the contents of my veins.
Because I was raised to become a King,
But here, it's often the Barbarian that reigns.
So maybe, it's time that I too went mad,
And started collecting heads for good measure.
Someone bring to me, my axe...
So that I may start swinging it with pleasure.

MOVE THE SCALES

In this space, brilliance doesn't matter.
For no matter how deeply still waters may run,
It is only the name beneath them that carries weight.
And ironically, for others,
Such as the selfish and unoriginal,
That name is meaningless.
They will take these images and present the words as
if they spawned them with their own hands.
Feigning eloquence in thought,
Even if they are painfully banal in deed.
So what are we to do? Are we to stop?
And let the words become dams within our veins?
Or do we stay the course,
And act as beacons for the ones we're meant to find?
I don't know anymore.
For I'm far too busy convincing myself,
That my name can even move the scales at all.

PROFOUND DENIALS

You say you want to read my words,
But your excuses are abound.
And your fear of confrontations help,
These denials feel profound.
But I'd rather hear your simple honesty
Dear, it needn't have to rhyme.
Instead you make my stomach turn
With your disingenuous pantomime.
I would rather you not say a word,
And maybe save your fucking breath.
Before it happens to escape,
Then introduce my attention span to death.

SCOTOMA

Nearing two decades worth of knowledge,
But it's said my observation's false.
So I must be barely breathing,
Are these thoughts lacking in their pulse?
Could I have been mistaken?
Was there nothing lurking in the grass?
Maybe it was scotoma?
Perhaps even my own reflection in the glass?
And yet here inside the summer breeze,
Are red flags waving just the same.
While I'm pretending not to notice,
Just to indulge the ones who play the game.
But how could they ever hope to fool the one
Who went broke from attention paid?
And used his pen to tuck them in
This self-righteous bed that they have made.
Maybe in the end some will learn,
Through these poignant lines that I have wrought.
But I know for some, these things must be felt
For the lessons to be lasting when they're taught.

WHERE THE WINDS ONCE LIVED

And he said unto her,
"You cannot move in and out of people's lives
As if you were the wind,
And expect them to rejoice on a windy day.
For there have been many of days
When their sail has stood proud,
And you were nowhere to be found.
Yet, here and now,
The proverbial seas are calm.
And you have the nerve to be mad,
Even dismayed, that the sail is drawn.
Oh, my beautiful and foolsh Aura...
If you're going to choose to come and go
You may as well be gone."

IN THE FIELDS

Life is but a field.
And in mine,
There are weeds masquerading as roses.
Showing their better sides,
Striking the all too familiar poses.
But after removing the blight
Of their blatant, false pretense.
I have simply chosen to erect a bigger fence.
To keep out the pretenders in the room.
And give my solitude the space
That it needs to truly bloom.
And still, this unattractive vine,
Continues searching for ways to grow.
For there are some who notice,
Yet pretend they didn't know.
But the most obvious things seem to sprout,
Where they are given the least amount of space.

WHEN THE FIREFLIES FADE

She used to speak of meditation.
She used to speak of fireflies.
Oh, she used to speak of so many things.
But now?
She doesn't speak at all.
And though a trace of pain still lingers;
Each passing day helps me to heal.
Despite every twist and turn of this town,
Reminding me of her own curves.
And despite this scorching, summer heat
Mirroring what she used to do to me;
The memories have begun to fade.
But on quiet nights like this,
The anger rises up to greet me.
And it asks,
"How could someone set a fire in me,
And not put it out before they left?"
But then I remembered...
She once spoke of fireflies.

LIFELINES

When a man is starving,
A morsel can seem like a feast
To eyes that want to close.
And in my weakened state,
Maybe I was too blind to see the truth:
I wanted something beautiful,
To hide the ugliness in me.
Too bad, I wasn't the only one
She looked at this way.
So by the time the smoke had cleared,
I learned that I was merely saving her from boredom;
As she pretended to rescue me from drowning.
I should've known that in the end,
Even lifelines don't come with loyalty.

IN THE DARK RECESSES

Like all slaves to the tides of time,
History repeats itself.
So it's not surprising when I tell you
The bells are ringing loudly in the tower.
But when I open up my eyes,
I realize it's my hand upon the rope.
Sensations I would've once died to feel now fade,
As they are drowned by the echoes.
They go without so much as a hint of a struggle.
What was once important,
No longer holds the same weight.
And from this vantage point,
Even kings and queens are the size of insects;
Proving we're all the same to the gods.
So all is right in the world.
A nation is in disarray.
Some souls are staring down the barrel
Of impending disasters.
And like all lepers,
I am exactly where I belong:
In the dark recesses.

THE BUTTERFLIES OF STOCKHOLM

Why is it that some butterflies
Yearn to be held within the jar?
Sure, they can then be seen by eveyrone
But now they can't travel very far.
But you see, I've learned
That it's in the storms of life,
Where the butterfly gets bruised.
And their wings become these heavy things,
That have only been abused.
And so they retreat;
Into the security and tranquility of captivity.
And the reason why is simple:
When all you have known is chaos,
Even solid ground begins to feel like prison.
And when minds are overrun with fear,
The butterfly doesn't factor logic,
Into its' poorly thought decision.

THE PRICE OF LEPROSY

To me, confidence is akin to credit.
How can you be expected to establish some,
If you are routinely turned down
When pursuing the things you want most in life?
They speak of these things
As if they are something
That you are supposed to already possess;
As if you were born with them.
But here in the bell tower,
The accounts are as empty as the halls I roam.
And it's only when this familiar song is sung,
That it comes to feel like home.
So what am I to do?
I guess I'll keep swiping in the fashion that I'm shown.
Maybe one day,
I'll end up with something of value,
That I can finally call my own.

THE FUMES OF PARANOIA

"Is something wrong?"
That is what they usually ask me.
I suppose my silence eats away at them;
Mirroring the way the doubts eat away at me.
Like an acid; burning away any trace of certainty.
Breathing in paranoia with the fumes.
Knowing full well,
That someone somewhere is hiding something from us.
And these truths that I know, need not be repeated.
For I see what looms on the horizon.
Daedalus warned me; and still I tempted fate
And now when the wax and feathers begin to rain,
Surely I cannot curse the sun
For doing what it was made to do.
Everything burns, my child.
A crazy man once said that.
But in troubled times like these,
I fear that he may have been on to something.

BLINDSIDED BY DESIRE

Deep in the wilderness of my mind,
We bear witness as anticipation reigns.
Desire is the king of all the beasts,
Being feared across the plains.
Every other thought that wanders stray,
Is blindsided and devoured.
And sadly, it's not just the body count
That keeps growing by the hour.
Concentration here is rare,
Much like storm clouds overhead.
For the heat just inspires thirst,
Just like when she is in my bed.
And so there's no escape for modest thoughts,
They'll find no solace in the shade.
For when the beast is drunk on lust,
Inhibitions will lead decorum to an early grave.
So I'd suggest these thoughts had better get on board,
Before they're introduced to teeth.
And they have no time to cry for help
When it's his majesty they're trapped and pinned beneath.
So when the King is on the prowl,
May the timid find the floor.
And when she reads my latest roar,
Let her know that yes, I'm demanding more.

WEARY BONES

Oh baby, I can see it in your eyes...
I know that you're tired.
The daily wars have left you drained;
And now you're looking for a soft place
To crash land your weary bones.
Because you don't have enough energy
To safely leave this pedestal I've put you on...
"You deserve better"
Became the mantra you'd always shout,
As I did my best to climb up and reach you.
But your defenses are too strong;
Repelling potential lovers like they were threats.
And much to my chagrin, you keep telling me what I need;
While ignoring that you're everything I want.
I believe you hold all of the keys
That will open all of the doors locked within me.
But it's of no use,
I fear your mind is already made up.
I swear I would be so good to you.
Yet in the end, good remains a slave to perspective.
And I am bound and chained, in my desires for you.

DUSK

Today is truly a beautiful day.
The sun is shining brightly,
Inside this Louisiana sky.
And yet, in my mind, it is dusk.
Depression is lurking just beyond each thought.
Ready to pour itself onto my disposition,
As if it were ink, to suffocate my joy.
And so, I do my damnedest to fight it.
Because I know that it was loneliness
That invited darkness to the party.
So I turn the music up, and begin to drive faster.
Hoping and praying that I can find a way,
To outrun the man behind the wheel.
For it is he, that is my greatest enemy.

BEHIND THE MASK

I stand here quietly in observation.
They flail and foment,
As they mistake my silence for timidity.
But this is how I learn;
This is how I see behind each of their respective masks.
For if given enough time,
People always show you who they really are.
Words are merely advertisements;
And actions are signposts...
That will lead you to the core of their characters.
And so many of them will always disappoint us.
Whether they profess to be unlovable
Because of previous damage,
Or whether they are truly a wolf
Wrapped in the wool of sheep;
The facade will slip in time.
And there I will be waiting.
With a blood-soaked and sharpened wit,
Lacking any mercy.
For I will not be betrayed again.

ANSWERED WITH SILENCE

We find ourselves in crazy times.
And all throughout history,
When society is spiraling out of control,
People will often turn to scripture.
Hoping that the ancient prophecies will help them to
understand the turbulence of the present.
And despite the great, red dragon
Swallowing the child of the virgin giving birth,
Nothing has noticeably changed.
But still, they swear the end is coming.
Yet in their eagerness to be called up,
They are dumbstruck to learn I don't believe as they do.
And when they ask me how I can live,
Without acknowledging their perceived creator,
I remind them that I wasn't always this way.
But eventually, I reached a point where I was tired
Of having my desperate prayers
Answered with silence.

CRIMSON WINGS

I can tell she's been through some things.
By the bright, red stains on her wings.
To me it seems, the rose can get lost in the weeds.
Forgetting it's room to grow that she needs.
And some will say her wounds are not real.
Yet they still will need time to heal.
For she must guard at all times how she feels.
Since it's hearts that bleed,
That are the best to steal.

THE SKY AWAITS

My father should've warned me...
"Son, once she's released
A caged bird with never long for another perch;
Much less another cage.
She will lose herself in the sky,
Long before you will ever see her again."
And as I recall those words,
The words that he never said...
I lost her in the light of the sun.
At least she was free now.

ELEMENTAL SIGNS

They claim the crabs come alive,
Beneath the light of the moon.
Prone to movements like the tides,
Revealing mysteries too soon.
Emotions are fluid,
When these passions are felt.
But the cards are not played,
In the manner they're dealt.
So the crab then retreats,
Deep down into its hole.
For it will only observe,
And then fight to regain control.
Yet despite wearing armor,
It can easily be killed.
When the holes in its heart
Continue going unfilled.

A SIMPLE TRUTH

At the risk of sounding cliché,
He wrote,
"You must remember
That it is our differences that makes us special.
And it is our similarities
That bring us happiness."
But sadly, the people were so busy
Being condescending and judgmental
That no one took the time to read his words.

WRAITH

My, how you mutilate yourselves...
Hopes and dreams are left bleeding out,
All because you couldn't avoid
The sharpened edges of your own expectations.
Foolish attempts,
At forcing others into molds they would never fit;
Or having them hyper-extend their arms,
Whilst reaching for brass rings they'd never get.
Oh, how you can be sadists in your search for love.
I laugh as you bludgeon each other with hardened hearts,
And expect only softness in return.
While declaring that every misstep is a lesson,
That most will never seem to learn.
But then you scream and fuck like primal things,
As if only banshees know of bliss.
And here I am beneath the blackened skies,
With nothing left to miss.
So I choose to wade into the dark,
Hoping to erode what's left of faith.
While demanding that my anger kill,
The memories of my every, gorgeous wraith.

SAFARI

I stumbled upon her,
As her heart was bleeding out upon the plains.
And I found myself fresh out of sympathy.
Apparently, she'd gotten lost on safari,
Becoming a victim of the majestic beast she sought.
Having long since tired of safety,
She wished for an element of danger.
So she foolishly tried to tame a lion in its element.
Thinking her love could coax the creature,
Into both submission and continued cooperation.
But she forgot lions are known to roam,
And have many prides that they consider home.
So now she's crying;
Wondering exactly where she went wrong.
Whilst singing to me the same, old tired song.
But instead of criticizing the lion for its behavior,
As I would've done in the past...
I decided to instead become one.
And so, I walked away.
Choosing to leave her bleeding out.
Just like a lion would.

WITH LOSS, COMES WISDOM

From a park bench, I saw a little girl crying.
Something else had caught her attention,
And when she looked back, she had lost her grasp on
the string of her balloon.
As it floated away, a little farther each second,
Her father knelt down to comfort her.
"I'm sorry, Daddy," she said, wiping her little eyes.
"Don't apologize for your wonder, baby."
He replied, while softly wiping her little face.
"Look at Daddy..."
"Don't ever apologize for being who you really are,
okay? Sometimes we lose the things we love, that's the
way the world works. It hurts, but I promise you that
the hurt doesn't last forever. And if this world can't
handle you as you are, then it doesn't deserve you."
And as the balloon disappeared into the sun,
I saw the little girl hug her father tightly,
As her carried her down the trail;
All the while, he was holding her mother's hand.
It was then, that I quickly remembered the profound
importance of truth in all of our lives.
Because sometimes, a father's words can water their
daughters like flowers.
For more often than not, with loss comes wisdom.

REFLECTIONS

In my desire to be kind,
I have often overlooked the obvious.
Knowing my own imperfections intimately,
I chalked your behaviors up as byproducts of struggles.
But now after watching you,
I realize that people are what they most often do.
You may try to present me with your best side,
But your actions betray those reflections.
And now, my instincts have gone into overdrive.
So my every interaction with you has been thoroughly
dissected; with a most, surgical precision.
Because despite your sweet words, and your professions
of love, you have proven that you cannot be trusted.
You are another predator posing as a house pet.
Ready to devour anyone who gets close enough to touch.
And then you'll have the audacity to blame others for
the solitude that you endure afterwards.
But people who are truly broken, they don't go around
screaming it to everyone; they simply lie in pieces and
hope that someone notices them.
You? You break yourself wide open,
Then pretend it's all of us who have the problem.

LITERAL PROVOCATION

Some take these words like roses,
And some take these words like knives.
But they're merely stout reflections of,
What goes on inside our lives.
So know that it's never been my intention,
To cause another soul to bleed.
My aim has been to merely plant a seed,
Or reach the catharsis that I need.
Yet still, they level accusations
That are unfounded in the least.
And so I'll be cast as the villain when,
This ink fashions me into a beast.
And I devour here upon the page,
Those who have incurred my rage.
Still I know I have done my best,
To keep it locked tightly in its cage.
But some see fit to throw their stones,
And provoke what lies within.
Then they'll have the nerve to wonder why
There is blood pouring from my pen.

THE HIGH COST OF LOVING

And here she comes again...
That one woman choir.
Singing that all too familiar song.
Asking for deliverance from heartache.
And yet, a heathen like me, can't help but wonder if
the angels have fallen deaf.
Does there come a point where forgiveness isn't
granted, after an action has been committed at least a
thousand times? For the angel in her always falls.
But never from grace;
Rather for the love of known sinners.
And because she does her best to do the work of the
gods, she lays down; opening those exquisite gates to
paradise. Making the most glorious room for yet
another silver-tongued serpent.
And while she is lost in this rapturous haze, she
forgets that salvation must be earned or asked for;
Never, ever given freely.
So, the story ends the same.
A modern day Eve is painted in the fashion of Lilith.
And her supposed Adam retires to his own devices.
Proving to all of us that the high cost of loving,
Is seldom worth the prices.

FOUNDATIONS

There she was...
So beautiful, so alive.
But little did the others know, she was dying inside.
Left neglected and alone, in her own home no less;
That place where love once used to live.
Yet behind the smiles, behind the clothes she wore so
well, I could see the blood.
Leaking from her broken heart.
And I imagined her perfect lips whispering tearful
prayers; to a God that never seemed to answer.
Still, friends with good intentions offered her well
wishes and recommendations of faith.
But I could see the questions in her eyes.
For I knew things that no man was supposed to
know; because she wore her hurt and her haunt like
this season's latest. And it makes me angry.
How can someone internally kill the one who would
die for them? And then it hits me like a brick;
Some men mistake their foundations for sidewalks.
And the fools wipe their shoes in the places they were
supposed to build their homes.
Leaving only damage in their wake.
And here I am, wishing her tearful eyes would've
noticed me...

- For Amanda

WHISPERS IN MY MEMORIES

Like most men, I can be a victim of my own pride.
Though it rarely rears its ugly head, my ego beats its
proverbial chest like war drums. As if these audible
platitudes, will result in the showering of attention. But it's
because of this, I am reticent to admit, that sometimes I too
need things. But the truth finds me at night; when the sun
has retired and the doubts come out to play. They remind
me just how much I need her. They taunt me, with her
whispers in my memories. Knowing full well, that to me,
her voice is a song without end. Medicinal in its tones, and
intoxicating in its melodies. Her voice is the only one that
should ever carry my name; this gifted sobriquet.
But in the end, the silence between us grows like weeds.
The greetings that once felt like roses have wilted, and all
that remains are the bittersweet recollections.
But I hold hope that one day the spring will come again,
and breathe new life into her desires;
Resurrecting the very reason that I breathe.
So that she may return, and take my breath away.

TRANSPLANT

If they only knew how tired I was...
Exhausted from trying to hold on to hope;
Despite it slipping through my hands like water.
And there she is... As beautiful as I remember.
Still claiming that she hates all of the attention;
Yet doing everything she can to get it.
Come to think of it, she must be tired too.
Those dichotomies can be so very hard to maintain.
But the few times she actually speaks to me,
Her words always seem to ring hollow.
Telling me how much I am missed,
Or just how much she loves my mind.
Some days, I wish she could transplant this mind into
a shell she'd actually find appealing;
Just so she could finally stop saying that.
Or at least then, I wouldn't have to fucking hear it.
But that's not the way the world works.
We, the overlooked, must make our homes
Within the mire and bell towers alike.
For we lepers belong out of sight;
And if she had her way, truly out of mind.

NEW ORNAMENTS

As I lie in bed, staring at the ceiling,
I am seething with anger.
If it were possible, I'm sure I would breathe smoke,
Just to get my point across.
I'm so tired of being the way that I am.
Giving everything to everyone, until it dwindles down
and leaves nothing for myself. When all they do, is spoon-feed
me lies, excuses, and the occasional, recycled compliment.
Their intentions no longer matter; for there is truth only in
their silence. And as this point, I would rather the silence, than
to ever see their fucking face again. Such sights once stained
my eyes and poisoned my mind with hope.
And that is the worst thing you can give to a man whom is
drowning between breaths: hope. He would much rather that
you simply threw him a rope. And after all of this time, I
thought I was giving them my own. Yet it turns out I was;
I just didn't see them wrapping it around my goddamn neck...
Until I found out that their idea of love,
Was to kick away the chair.
And let me become their new ornament for the holidays.

END OF ACT 2

"Nothing has such power to broaden the mind as the ability to investigate systematically and truly all that comes under thy observation in life."

- Marcus Aureilus

"It is necessary to look at the results of observation objectively, because you, the experimenter, might like one result better than another."

- Richard P. Feynman

3
REVELATIONS

"What then do you call your soul?
What idea have you of it? You cannot of
yourselves, without revelation, admit the
existence within you of anything but a power
unknown to you of feeling and thinking."

- Voltaire

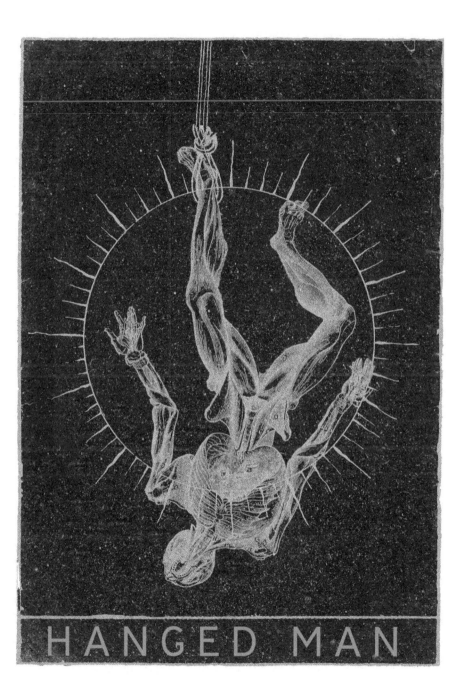

POMPEII

Note to self... Move next time.
What were you thinking?
How could you just stand there?
Like a deer in headlights.
No one escapes these situations unscathed.
You can't stand on the outskirts of the city,
And just watch as Pompeii begins to burn.
Did you actually think you'd escape the fire?
Molten death is pouring through the streets;
And there you are, trying to play the hero.
As if their stories couldn't turn into tragedies.
As if those with good intentions, couldn't turn into ash.
Please, self...
For the love of anything and everything,
Just stay out of it next time.
Take your stance on much higher ground.
Crosshairs don't discriminate,
And thrown stones don't negotiate.
No one wins in the end.
And while the survivors may give you flowers,
They will be on your casket;
And not in your hand.

ENJOY THE FALL

For years, my kindness was taken for weakness.
As if the open hand that I extended,
Was an offensive gesture,
In a culture that I was never exposed to before.
But in retrospect, I was weak.
Not for being kind to others.
But for not being kind to myself.
I destroyed myself with both words and deeds.
Denigrating my own worth.
Because its value wasn't seen by others.
It's not their fault that they're blind.
It's not their fault that they know not what they do.
The last great thing they've seen, was nailed to a cross.
And I've since learned the truth.
Society always kills those who try to help them.
Whether it was on Mount Calvary,
Or a balcony in Memphis,
They always kill their betters.
And maybe it's time I stopped being better.
Maybe it's time to get down and dirty,
Start living like the fallen.
After all, if I start pretending to have a little fun,
I may end up having some by accident.

FLOOD FOR THOUGHT

Remember, dear…
"If you keep praying for rain,
One day,
The streets are going to flood.
Then you'll have to explain to everyone
Without an ark,
Why they deserved the mud."

RAVENOUS HEARTS

It is easy to find the beauty in a want.
And yet,
It's hard to hide the ugliness in a need.
But when the heart is ravenous,
It's up to us to decide,
Which mouth of the monster we shall feed.

BONFIRES & BURDENS (PART I)

The truth has become apparent to me.
As if the veil was lifted, and the weights fell from my
eyes like the scales of Saul.
I know now what I must do.
Some are meant to find their place inside the light,
While others are meant to navigate the night.
I believe I am the latter.
For I never feel at home beneath the sun.
No, it is the moon that bids my tired feet to end their
run. And so, I must wander these roads alone.
Certain of both who I am, and more importantly,
who I am not. And I will never be the man who
burns his bridges, and then wonders why he is alone
beside the bonfires.
No, I am the man for whom decency has become a
burden; and pleasure a most pointless of pursuits.
But still, I push forward, into the wind.
For I endure.

BONFIRES & BURDENS (PART 2)

Decency is a burden
In a world where only the wicked seem to prosper.
Whether you believe it is at the hands of men or the
gods, we are moved as pawns all the same.
We exist below ceilings made of glass,
Hoping to one day reach through them, and reach
proverbial rings made of brass.
Most of us come from modest means, and inherit only
debts, instead of wealth. We put constraints on our
own lives, based solely off of societal pressures.
But in those moments, nothing of substance is forged.
And so we wait.
For a retirement financed by the lottery. For a savior's
return, to a corner of the world we are taught to fear.
For some fleeting form of fame, to pluck us from the
grips of obscurity. But nothing ever comes to rescue us.
So we continue living our lives; smiling.
Hoping to both hide from governments, and hide from
each other, while we mask our quiet desperation.

MAN OR MAELSTROM

I owe you an apology, dear. It seems rubber boots, nor rubber coats, could adequately prepare you for the mess that I am. After all was said and done, I'm sure you asked yourself, if I was a man or a maelstrom. And the truth is, I am both; just not impressive in either form. I huffed and I puffed, but my winds brought no change. My eyes rained and rained, but washed away no sins. My bitter fires scorched the Earth; but like fools, left the ground unfit for growth. My sword still lies trapped in stone; waiting for a worthy hand to come along, and wake it from its slumber. But alas, they have been few and far between. And so, I rage in the darkness; internally fueled and malcontent. I expect no visitors here in the tower. For the days are dark enough to see the stars. And the nights are so bleak, the moon no longer shows herself. But that's fine; her phases leave me unfazed. Still, I rage, and I wait. One day the churning will cease, and I'll finally be free of this beast. It has crowded my bedroom mirror for far, far too long.

A LIGHTHOUSE DARKENED

I've recently discovered a profound truth about myself.
One that I've been told a thousand times; yet, my denials
rang too loudly. But they were right: I am too nice. It is a
crushing realization. But you already knew that, didn't
you dear? Because, for you, I am the lighthouse. When
the seas become too turbulent, and your latest captain has
abandoned ship, that is when you seek my glow.
Fluttering your eyes, as if to say, "it's that time again,
won't you show me the way?" So my arms become the
safe harbor, that you swim to reach. The place to rest
your weary and water-soaked bones. And like the fool
that I am, I laid out like a welcome mat. But now that I
know my problem, it can be corrected. So next time,
when your life begins to capsize and you flutter your
pretty eyes, I will instead watch you drown. And then you
will know how I feel, while standing here on dry land,
shining my light to the undeserving and the blind.

ALCHEMIST AT HEART

I am an addict of sorts.
Going through withdrawls in silence.
Still using every opportunity I can get,
To chase that creative high.
The one that hits you,
When you bend words to your will.
But in truth, I am an alchemist at heart.
Hoping to use my mind, heart, and soul
As the places where I can transmute ink
Into true gold, using a pen guided by The Stone.
Knowing that there are those who read,
And remember that the world wasn't going to end.
At least not today.
Knowing there are those who prefer
The simplicities of life,
But they are unaware they are worthy of worship.
They just haven't found the person
Who sees the diamonds within them.
But they are out there.
Mining for hope.Waiting for them.
And maybe even, writing this.

SUCCUMB

In silence, he sought some understanding.
But there was none to be found.
So he looked up to the sky,
In his search for solid ground.
But suggestions continued coming,
To erode the progress he had made.
As he fought to bury all the memories
And use his frustrations as a spade.
But there's silence in the gallery,
As this disaster is slowly framed.
Even the lost succumb to vanity,
When their masterpiece is named.
By our tendency to paint ourselves as martyrs
In the stories that we tell.
Strong enough to bear the crown of thorns,
We've learned to wear so well.

UNEARTHED

There is no ink inside my veins;
And still, I bleed upon the page.
Whether it is done as testiments to lust,
Or lines blinded by my rage.
My heart adorns my sleeve,
As a symbol you should heed.
As proof, there's a drive behind my eyes,
To unearth these expressions that you read.
I'm compelled to tell the world,
Of these delightful things I think.
As if they're couplets imprisoned in my mind,
That escape each and every time I blink.
You know nothing of the pain,
That comes with baring souls.
Nor do you know the pain of revelations,
When your hands are not on the controls.

OVERPOWERED

Listen.
Do you hear that?
That's the sound of nothingness.
A silence so profound,
I could toss a stone or coin,
And never hear it hit the ground.
For it would be like me;
Forever falling.
Without anything or anyone to catch it.
And I'd be lying if I said I've never been here before.
Hell, you'd think I'd be used to it by now.
One would assume I would quit lowering my guard,
Like an empty pail,
Since I knew that all the wells had run dry.
No, I gave into foolish hopes again.
Forgetting that giving second chances,
Only leaves room to be disappointed twice.
And sadly, I truly expected this from the start.
But that's what happens,
When the head is overpowered by the heart.
One of them bleeds.

SELECTIVE VISION

Myopia tends to blur the vision,
When gazing at the stars.
How can light from so long ago,
Burn twice as bright as ours?
But I guess that doesn't matter now,
Oh, you've made sure of that.
Creators spill their ink atop the sky,
Turning all my brightest days to black.
But you can get used to things,
When they occur with frequency.
And it's the things we need the most,
That we fail to even see.
For our eyes tend to wander,
To things we've been denied.
And things that don't belong to us,
Make us extend our arms with pride.
Oh, we covet all our neighbor's goods
And envy his grass that's always green.
Like a motion picture behind a fence,
That plays out so serene.
But then reality comes crashing in,
And we slowly peer behnd the mask.
Denying that selective vision makes us blind,
We claim it just depends on who you ask.

MY ADVICE IS DROWN

I am so very far from perfect.
One glance at me,
And that is all it takes to reach that conclusion.
But these days, it is hard to mask my disappointment.
So many people are not who I thought them to be.
And this recipe for disaster,
Is both equal parts comedy and tragedy.
So what do you do?
When what you perceived as a diamond in the rough,
Is nothing more than a rhinestone
In the center of a mess they made themselves?
Do you laugh? Do you cry?
Do you carry on about your days,
Hoping to escape the gravity of their maelstrom?
Or do you buckle down,
And venture past their event horizon?
I honestly don't have the answers, my friend.
For each situation is different.
But in this case,
When a fool is drowning in metaphors,
I wouldn't waste a rope.
I would much rather throw them a cinder block.

COLLECTING DUST

Love itself isn't evil;
But people most certainly can be.
You see, people are fickle.
Their wants and desires are often fluid.
Some of us have the ability to bend with the wind,
Yet never break our overall convictions.
Whereas some don't value themselves enough
To stand firm where they find stability.
No, they find comfort in the chaos.
But as I always say,
While experiences in life may have broken some people,
I lost my patience for making mosaics long ago.
The rewards have never been worth the effort for me.
I have enough goddesses displayed,
Here in the museum of my mind.
The last thing I'd need,
Is to add to a collection that rarely does anything
Except collect the dust from their passing memories.

WHETSTONES

Some people are pathetic in their pursuits.
Selfish little shits that flail about,
Leaving nothing of merit within their wake.
And some people understand that.
So they forgive and they forget.
But I say fuck that!
Because people like me?
We use memories as whetstones.
To sharpen every word,
Until I can throw lines that feel like blades.
And if you were here now,
I would plunge this one between your ribs.
Just to ask you how Christ felt upon the cross.
As you were gasping for air,
Knowing that you would drown without water.
Then I'd whisper in your ear,
"Now you know how it feels."
But worry not, little martyr.
These are but thoughts. Your wretched soul is safe.
For there is no justice in this world.
Just monsters hidden beneath make-up.
And bitter kings throwing daggers from a distance.

LITTLE REMINDERS

There are times when the wolf in me
Tires of howling at the moon.
The only replies I hear,
Are the echoes being strangled by distance.
They slowly become whispers that suffer in vain,
So that silence may once again rule the night.
But it's this truth, that makes me bare my teeth.
Wanting to go on the hunt for fate,
So that I may lunge and tear its throat out.
Leaving only the moon to witness my blood-soaked jaws,
Reuniting between the laughs.
Biting down with purpose until the deed is done;
And there are only red footprints on the ground.
Little reminders...
That it's unwise to hunger,
Those you have no intention of feeding.

WHEN LIONS BECOME LAMBS

In this life, I have learned a brutal lesson.
Both through observation and experience.
You must never give your all to a lover.
For things will always run their course.
And after time, even royalty will tire of gold.
You must save something for yourself.
So if they decide to leave,
They don't carry the best of you with them.
And having said that,
I must now heed my own advice.
For I've always placed my heart upon my sleeve.
And like the weather,
Her love is ever-changing and unkind.
I guess when the goddesses are selfish,
And they demand a sacrifice
Even lions can become lambs,
That will surely pay the price.

BESTOWED TO CHANCE

I believe that God is just the name
That we've bestowed to chance.
Unaware that His angels are instead the odds,
We seek to curry favor in the dance.
But like those who've come before us,
We're at the mercy of the sands.
And there'll come a day when the game will end,
It's a truth nobody wants to understand.
No, they believe they'll carry on
And get to see behind the veil.
Once the house their soul is living in,
Has fallen cold and pale.
But I feel that point of view,
Fails to see the beauty in the now.
They're so obsessed with groveling,
Since there's a book that taught them how.
But friend, I would rather live my life,
As if tomorrow was never guaranteed.
For I know only sleep awaits for me,
And today, she's the only Heaven I will ever need.

ESCAPE CLAUSE

Everyone always has advice to spare.
But I've had my fill of such nonsense.
I'd say to anyone listening:
Offer yourself to no one.
They will only take what they can.
Then once they get bored,
They will find another soul to feed on.
See? Most people act as if their crisis is existential;
But it's all just a show.
Everyone knows exactly what they're doing.
Every decision is made with a result in mind.
The weak put themselves under the infulence,
To give themselves an excuse.
An escape clause.
While the strong do whatever we want,
And take the secrets to our graves.
So in the end, fuck worrying about other people.
Live for yourself.
Don't bother losing blood or tears,
By trying to mend the broken.

SAND IN THE WIND

They say the devil
Has made an art form out of tempation.
And they say that the Lord
Has salvation down to a science.
But me? My beliefs keep evolving.
All I know for certain,
Is that the sun will rise tomorrow,
And one day I won't.
So until that day, darling
Don't waste my fucking time.
If you want me, say it. And I'm yours to enjoy.
If you don't, that's cool too.
There's no need to feign sadness, baby.
Bad taste isn't a capital crime.
Just don't look for me to chase you, though.
Once I lose interest in you,
You might as well be sand in the wind.
For I've spent too many nights in my own head,
Overturning stones.
And I've spent too many days,
Trying to decipher mixed signals.
And I've lost my patience for both.
So the next person that tells me
They know how to swim,
Better be ready to fucking drown.

THINLY VEILED

I can see that look in your eyes.
It's happening again, isn't it?
The withdrawals?
Those pains that make your veins feel like chains.
Burdens to be worn,
As they bulge and bring you down.
But fear not, my darling.
Your favorite dealer has returned.
With some new lines for you to do more,
Than just read between.
Then? There was no need to roll your dollar bills.
Now? My newest collection has arrived.
But these were just intended to be morsels,
For your inner addict to abuse, baby.
Since this is the only way that I can earn your gaze.
I have to jot it down and leave it thinly veiled,
So you can enjoy it in your haze.
But intentions never matter,
Only results will stand the test of time.
So I'll keep chipping away at your defenses,
And before you know it,
I'll be deep inside you with a rhyme.

THE SUMMIT

It was at a young age, that I first learned of death.
And as I grew into being a man,
I would discover that I was dead inside.
But strangely, it was in a supermarket parking lot
That I would come to learn of resurrection.
Because that is where she kissed me for the first time;
And brought me back to life.
And so, while life has shown me peaks and valleys
Since then, my heart hasn't always come along
With me throughout the journey.
'Cause when it gets hurt by the things I witness,
I find that it retreats back to that parking lot.
Looking for her.
Hoping to be healed by its owner.
And it's then, that the truth hit me.
Most people don't want to climb,
Because they fear the fall.
But me? I don't climb,
Because I've already reached the summit.
And I didn't realize it,
Because it looked just like a parking lot.

THE FIRES OF LIFE

To some, it will always be more attractive
To try and solve the mystery of who provided the
spark for the passion in my words, than it is to ever
try and change the reality behind them.
Sadly, some would rather be immortalized
And left to be the envy of the world,
Than to be placed alongside me
In the fires known as life.
For those like me know the flames are transformative,
And they will spare no one.
They will harden some like steel, and allow them to
endure the years of solitude to come.
And others, the flames will make beautiful,
But fragile as if they're made of glass.
So it's no surprise when they run,
As soon as the temperature rises.
They're too afraid to break.
And all the while,
I am beyond tired of burning alone.

IDLE HANDS

I would say that I'm surprised
But at this point, it would be a lie.
I examine each new thing I learn,
And I find my wonder dies a little more each time.
I reconcile this painful truth
With these secrets that I shouldn't know,
And there's only indifference in its' wake.
For the things that belong to me,
Are only ever owned in thought.
Possession is merely a fluid state of being.
And after a while, even the thirsty will tire of trying to
hold water in their hands.
Because this type of bliss is momentary, you see?
Eventually, all good things run their course.
Leaving idle hands,
To know this emptiness I've lived.
And so some days,
I ask myself why do I even bother to breathe?
But then I remember...
There is much work to be done.

VOLUMES UNHEARD

I'd be lying if I said I wasn't nervous.
The culmination of years of work,
Is once again waiting in the wings.
Like some beast pacing behind a locked door;
Waiting with bated breath,
For its' chance to finally run.
So many tell me, I should be excited.
So many others tell me, I should be proud.
And to be truthful, I love them all for saying so.
But in the end,
The silence is much louder than the collective.
For it's in my quiet times,
That the roars grow the loudest.
And that is when I fear the doors will open,
And the object of their wonder will fall flat upon its' face.
Having stumbled out of the gate.
Leaving all of this, to have been for naught.
Yet, in the end, I can truly rest knowing
That this is the second volume that bears my name.
Even if it goes unheard.
For often times,
Art with meet the fate of its' creators:
They'll simply collect dust for awhile.

HAUNTED

My life is far from perfect;
Yet, despite my cynicism,
I believe that perfection exists.
I was lucky enough to taste it twice.
The first time was ever so briefly.
And the second,
Was for much longer than I deserved.
But now this empty bed feels like a precipice.
And though I project this image of apathy,
The truth isn't hard to see: I am haunted.
Memories have built a home inside my heart,
And the ghosts of goddesses roam these empty halls.
Retracing the footsteps they left in their wake.
And I'm here, trying to get high
On their perfume I can no longer smell.
Knowing full well,
That a life spent without either of them,
Is the closest thing to hell.

SHADOW FOREST

Life is but a wilderness.
Sometimes we bask in the shade that we find
In the welcoming shadows of giants.
But other times,
We are frightened to be so far off the beaten path;
So far away from our comfort zones.
But we know that it's just beyond their edges,
That greatness has been said to lie.
And so we go forth; drenched in trepidation.
Because there is always a risk
When venturing into the unknown alone.
For some souls, true discoveries may lead to martyrdom.
And yet for others,
Their search may bring them just rewards.
I find that the results depend on where you stand
During the unveiling of these revelations.
Because we all long to see the forest,
And not just the trees.
And the light brings with it judgment,
That is why the shadows put most of us at ease.

DAWN'S BREAK

Here it is... Another sleepless night.
My face lies still;
Bathed in the neon of a foreboding alarm clock.
A brutal reminder, that in just a few hours,
The soul crushing will begin.
And that is why I have come to dread the break of
dawn; for it is then that I must report back to work.
I must forgo all poetic inclinations,
And all desires for creative expressions;
So that I may work like an efficient, mindless drone.
Punching clocks and trading each minute of my life
that passes for pennies on the dollar.
I believe that we weren't meant to live this way.
We were meant to greet the morning sun as the
Kings and Queens of our respective worlds.
But instead, we've become soulless machines;
Indentured slaves to the means
That help us acquire our ends.
Will we ever find a way
To salvage our inner light before it's too late?

WINDS OF CHANGE

Like grains of sand,
Our expectations are subject to the winds of change.
No matter how well we believe them to be planted in
reality, because of the fluid nature of life, hopes and
dreams so very rarely take root.
So it is because of this, that we must draw inspiration
from the often overlooked bamboo.
Its rigidity gives it strength;
But its flexibility gives it grace.
And so it will bend without breaking;
Allowing it to go with the flow,
Without losing its foundation.
It's amazing how the bamboo offers so much wisdom to
those who hear what can only be observed.
And that is how we all must be, my friend.
We must be willing to throw ourselves into the wind,
Instead of fortifying our lives against its power.
Because greatness is rarely found,
In the bunkers shaped like comfort zones.

HOURGLASS

I once heard that closed mouths will never get fed;
Yet, I've learned through trial and error,
That open books will never get read.
Because it's things that are discovered,
That will become a part of lore.
And it's things that are presented,
That will introduce an interest to a bore.
A man must first strive and forge himself,
Into a highly, treasured find.
For there is not a scarcity upon the shelves,
So one must be made inside her mind.
See? I could tell the world so many things,
Layered deep within a rhyme.
But I know she'd rather have me build a watch,
Than to simply tell the current time.
Because she knows that men are clocks,
That rush with overzealous hands.
And so she longs to love an hourglass,
Whom will always catch his falling sands.
You must let her build her monuments,
Where there once was only stones.
And in turn, she'll feel a desire so profound,
It will burn your name into her bones.

OLD ORNAMENTS

Friend, I fought to maintain my composure;
But exuberance convinced me otherwise.
And so, I told her exactly how I felt;
But my words were left hanging in the air.
Like some old, unwanted ornaments to be returned.
Seemingly upset, she showered me with silence.
And in return, indifference slowly drowned my anger.
The reason being, that this is no one's fault but my own.
I seem to always do this to myself.
I have long since poured my heart out to the
undeserving. It comes to them like waterfalls,
While they are merely holding plastic cups, remember?
They are unprepared for all that I wish to give.
And so I've learned, that the volume of a gift
Will never increase its value,
In the eyes of those who never saw you in the first place.
So save yourself the trouble.
Hoard your love.
Until a soul proves themselves to be worthy.

DOUBLE-EDGED SWORD

I've discovered that this heart that adorns my sleeve
Is, quite frankly, a double-edged sword.
Every time it has been unsheathed
In an effort to draw love from another,
I have only ever drawn blood from myself.
It was then, that you'd come around,
Using broken records as tourniquets.
Offering excuses draped in pleasantries;
As feeble and facetious attempts to stave my bleeding.
You'd always tell me how I deserved better than this,
Before pointing me in a direction
That was anywhere except beside you.
And that is fine.
I've always known that I may not set fires in everyone.
But then you'd have to audacity,
To tell me how I should feel about the one inside of the
proverbial looking glass.
And you've quite clearly lost your goddamned mind.
You don't get to cast souls away,
Like stones across a lake,
And then tell them to ignore the ripples you've made in
their reflection.
So why don't you do us both a favor,
And go crawl back up on your cross?
Since it seems like you're always the martyr in your
own stories... Just like I am.

SELF-RIGHTEOUS

They say He healed the blind,
And helped the wayward and the meek.
He journeyed through the countryside,
Drawing crowds whenever He would speak.
He even called himself Messiah,
Despite knowing exactly what it would cost.
Some claimed He walked on water,
Yet they still nailed Him to a cross.
But fast forward to the present,
And some will use His name in vain.
When others share their struggles,
Some of His believers just complain.
Still, they quote the good book
Whilst paraphrasing His every word.
But if you're missing empathy,
Was it really His message that you heard?
For if you see another bleeding,
And you fail to lend a hand.
You've proved that devils do exist,
When good men fail to take a stand.
So while I may be a nonbeliever,
And those flames will be my home.
I refuse to be a fucking coward,
Or a soul with a heart of stone.
So please don't speak to me of Jesus,
As if you think that will tip the scales.
Because it was the Romans who may have killed Him,
But it was the self-righteous that held the nails.

THE WORST FEELING

Today, I have discovered
The absolute, worst feeling in the world.
And it's because now when I see her,
After we embrace...
Her eyes say,
"How have you been?"
They no longer say,
"I've missed you."
And that kills me inside.
So I do my best to smile,
Instead of bleed.

IN THE CLOUDS

Growing up,
I spent most of my time
With my head lodged in the clouds.
I was always wishing, wondering, and dreaming.
Imagining exciting lives I'd never lead,
And gorgeous souls I'd never get to love.
But that's life.
It doesn't always work out the way you wish.
Nowadays, I rarely venture outside of this bell tower.
But when I do, I seem to find a way to screw things up.
Whether it's misinterpreting signs meant for my eyes
alone, or not deserving the pedestal I was briefly placed
upon, I both fall and fail often.
Maybe I should remain in this tower,
Until all that would be left of me is my remains.
Because everything feels like a burden.
A burden made heavier by breathing.
I would ask for forgiveness,
But it seems I'm far too tired to grovel.

THIRD EYE

She spoke to me of ancient wisdom,
But made it modern in a sense.
Sincerity held her every word,
So there was no room for false pretense.
She said our voices held the power,
To turn vibrations into law.
So we should only speak of wonders,
And things that enrapture us in awe.
Because if we only spoke of darkness,
If would find us all in time.
And we speak the tragic into existence,
If there is doubt within our rhyme.
So I should square my shoulders back,
And speak as if I were a King.
And the universe would answer me,
As if a bell were made to ring.
Oh, she is wise beyond her years
So her counsel is often sought.
For she knows the greatest things in life,
Are seldom ever bought.
And though her light could rival suns,
She's more alive beneath the moon.
So she often wanders to the shore,
To let the tides serenade her with a tune.
And as they crash down upon the toes,
She has softly buried into sand.
I wonder if she knows that I am grateful,
That she helped me to understand...
That to become the man I wish to be,
My Third Eye must be made to see.

- For Dena

"THE WAKING LION" ART BY VALISA BERNARDINO

THE NATURAL ORDER

Mask the emptiness with laughter,
In valiant attempts to win the war.
Slaughter subtle joys like they were cattle,
And pretend they were never felt before.
Then gravitate toward indifference,
Leave not a soul to blame.
Let actions provide examples,
That beliefs were consecrated all the same.
And as you sanitize your new perspective,
Wear leather gloves to hold the line.
As baited hooks entice the weak,
To enjoy being sacrificed in time.
For circumstances may lead to questions,
About the righteousness of cause.
But these lambs were made for subjugation,
So the lion must never hesitate or pause.
They must embrace the natural order,
Once they've awakened the inner beast.
Sure, consequences can be ugly,
But they're a necessary element for peace.
So assuage the guilt that comes in waves,
By knowing that preservation is the key.
To unlocking all the doors,
And truly remaining free.

BEASTS OF BURDEN

The adepts and initiates, they call us beasts of burden.
They see us as steaks upon their plates,
Waiting to be devoured.
Unfit to rule ourselves. Unaware of our own ignorance.
Unaware of their ever-growing power.
So many of us lulled into comfort and sleep,
By gossip rags and flashing screens.
But that's just how they want it.
Even if you run to your nearest pew,
You still won't escape their grasp.
Your saviors are considered mere perversions of their
ancient mysteries.
They own everything we eat, see, and hear.
They've spread like a virus through our collective red,
white, and blue bloodstream.
And they were right: I am a beast.
Sharpening my mind as well as my fangs.
Burdened with a knowledge,
I intend to share before it's too late.
Before I end up like all of the other messengers,
Who have met a truly, grizzly fate.
All speakers of truth end up disgraced or murdered.
That's why so many choose to live a lie.
But if that's the case,
I would much rather stand for something before I die.

EXOTERIC DESIRES

In the olden times, they would say
That I have been weighed and found wanting.
But would they had eyes to see,
This truth was never held as a rite of passage.
No, this revelation has always been exoteric.
Yet, in all honesty, this doesn't matter in the long run.
Men far greater than I have always been held sway by the
things they cannot understand or possess.
The allure of the unattainable is too much for mere mortals.
The low-hanging fruit may as well be bitter,
To we seekers of the climb.
And from that vantage point, one could easily see,
That there are some things in this world worth the effort.
And believe me, dear friend...
She is worth everything and more.
Her eyes could make the oceans recede in envy.
Her kiss can heal wounds that have gone unseen.
Her touch can inspire the weak and humble the proud.
And her name is the greatest thing I have ever said aloud.
So do not ask me why I wait for her.
For some things are worth dying for;
Even if it must happen in slow motion.

SECRETS OF THE TRADE

Would you like to know a secret, my friend?
In this profane world of ours, magic does exist.
I have seen it with my own eyes.
I know you will doubt my words;
But hear me, I beg you.
Magic resides at that perfect point,
Where belief and illusion collide.
Knowing this, a true magician never reveals their secrets.
For their power lies in their ability to breathe into the
impossible, and give it tangibility.
Thus, sparking inside your mind, the fires of wonder.
Reducing your cynical mind to ashes,
And allowing your inner child to sift through the dust that
gives this life meaning.
But you knew this already; albeit subconsciously.
The truth is, you want to be fooled. We all do.
That's why we believe our partners
When they tell us that they love us.
It's why we believe them,
When they give us reasons for pushing us away.
Like children, we simply want to believe in magic.
But our minds won't let us.

SOUNDTRACK FOR THE DAMNED

Standing at the edge of all I've held dear,
I reach out into the void.
Far beyond restraints and comfort zones,
Hoping to feel as misconceptions are destroyed.
But no matter how often I extend my hands,
They return as empty as before.
So this is where the mind retreats to doubt,
And finds comfort in their lore.
Yet fairy tales bring no solace, friend;
For they ring hollow every time.
They lead us far away from reasoning,
With every contradiction in the lines.
Still so many cling to them,
As if they're capsized and adrift.
Thinking tribulation will prepare them for
The enjoyment of an eternal gift.
And as the rest of us are left to burn,
They'll say we deserve no less than flames.
As echoed screams and searing flesh,
Provide a soundtrack for the pain.

THE AGE OF SADNESS

Prometheus paid a heavy price,
For the things he gave away.
And for centuries Pandora bore the blame,
For the sins we face today.
Then dear Achilles finally fell,
When weakness learned his name.
And Samson lost his source of strength,
When Delilah played her wretched game.
But now I fear Medusa's seen my heart,
Since it's feeling more like stone.
We've watched Atlas hold up the world,
As I've fought to hold my own.
But I feel my shoulders start to shake,
As sweat falls inside my hands.
It takes so much effort to maintain,
Yet nobody ever understands.
That in the myths of yesterday,
Few things were seldom proven true.
But as you watched me hold my world,
You knew I dreamed of holding you.
Still you often turned away,
Choosing another to have your love.
And so I'm left with the sadness of the age,
That I cannot rise above.
My, how I empathize with the gods...

UPON THE PAGE

In the dead of the night,
I often find myself awake,
And dying upon the page.
Hopelessly trying to find
The right combination of words
That will not only
Change lead into gold,
But the phrase that just maybe
Could bring her back to me.

SOME DAYS

Some days I actually wish,
That I never knew your name.
Some days I'm here missing you,
Without an ounce of shame.
Some days I wish we could go back,
To the way it used to be.
And then there are days like today,
When I wish you were there missing me.

HER, PART I: THE PAST

If you look at her past
Like it was a cocoon,
Do you really have to wonder
Why she is so damn beautiful now?

HER, PART 2: THE TRUTH

Through the power of her faith,
Courage blossomed within her heart;
Allowing the truth to grow wings upon her tongue.
And be born into freedom with each breath.
She now speaks without fear.
May those in power, learn to tremble before her.
For she will never be silenced again.
Mark her words.

HER, PART 3: THE LOOK

People often have a habit of speaking to her,
As if they actually understand her.
As if by bearing witness to her days,
They could actually walk a mile in her heels.
But let me be the first to tell you, they couldn't.
Because when the world applies pressure to her,
She stands firm and does not break.
When the weather brings to her only storms,
She endures and does not bend.
And when the actions of others cause her pain,
She may bruise; but rest assured she will not bleed.
So now you tell me,
Has defiance ever looked better?

HER, PART 4: THE DANGER

When it comes to love,
There is much a woman will give;
And there is much a woman will take.
But what she will not allow,
And what she will not be.
Is taken for granted.
So be careful with a woman
Whom has seemingly reached her breaking point...
For there is nothing in this world more dangerous,
Than a woman with a point to prove.

HER, PART 5: THE UNIVERSE

Eventually, she discovers the truth:
That beneath all of her struggles,
Far below all of her self-doubt,
Even further past what was done to her,
There is more to her than pain!
There is divinity exploding within her!
To one lucky soul, she will become the world.
But to those with eyes to see?
She is the very universe itself.
Sculpted by the hand of our Creator,
And given breath to delight us all.
So now I must ask, is she not magnificent?
Is she not worthy of reverence and worship?
Has there ever been a better name upon my tongue,
Than her? My sweet Esmeralda...

HER, PART 6: IN THE END

Through this pen,
I have discovered many things about her.
My absolute favorite thing is her gratitude.
Has there ever been someone more thankful to be alive,
Than a survivor?
I'm sure I would be hard-pressed to find one.
Yet, she refuses to brag upon her own strength.
For she wears humility as if it were designer clothes.
And with each layer she unravels before me,
I cannot help but to be in awe.
Because I've learned, that all she really wants is peace.
Though her sword and shield are never far from reach,
She is ready to lay the rest of her armor down.
And as someone fighting his own war, I can relate.
So I pray to all of the gods,
That the arrows stop flying inside her mind.
And I pray that she rediscovers exactly how it feels...
To once again love herself.
Because the gods know, that I still love her.

WAR DRUMS

I knew my desire was dead,
When I looked at your picture
And neither Heaven nor
The Earth began to move.
For a heart that was once
The envy of war drums,
Now mirrors the still waters
In the clichés you used to say.
You've proven that silence is golden,
Only when the subject becomes worthless.

SAVE THE DROWNING

In moments of weakness,
My hands reach out for you;
And they return with nothing
But memories.
In moments of clarity,
I finally accept the truth:
Even the best of life-preservers
Have no use on dry land.

THE WILLING MARTYR

Where once I saw only
Queens and Goddesses,
Now I see only mortals.
Where once I was blinded
By pedestals and possibilities,
Now I see only patterns.
And where I once played
The willing martyr,
Now I see only thieves
Beside me on the cross.
For you have reduced
My every sacrifice to loss.
And you have dressed
Each of my resurrections,
As nothing more than
Lessons I left unlearned.

WHISPERS OF REVOLUTION

I fear when all is said and done
History will not speak highly of us
In the generations to come.
For they will read our words,
And know that we did not agree
With the tyrants of the day;
But when they look toward our actions,
They will ask themselves,
"Why didn't you ever try to stop them?"
And in turn, they will see
Our cries for revolution
As nothing more than whispers...

ISLAND OF SORROWS

I have become an island unto myself.
Having capsized into nameless seas,
And been drowned by the weight
Of misguided expectations.
I now find myself pondering
If the supine nature I have developed,
Could make these messages I bottle and release,
Any more well-received.
In the end, I know full well
The fate that awaits me.
And as the tides crash down,
Stealing parts of me ever so discreetly,
I feel nothing but acceptance.

WHEN DARKNESS BLOOMS

Like the peppered moth,
I have watched you change over the years.
Your fastidious visage
Merely an offered boon to those around you.
While the invisible are left to see the truth:
When the sun goes down,
The darkness has a way of finding us all.
You thought yourself immune to such a fate.
Yet the silence you thrust upon me
Still speaks volumes, darling.
And now that the land
Has been bathed in soot and ash,
You long for the days
When you observed the birds;
Not the other way around.

PRISONERS OF THE MIND

Generation after generation
The shackles remain unseen.
Still, they are passed down,
Without thought or contestation.
For they believe their imprisonment
To be of the moral standing.
As if their knees were made
To do nothing but bend.
I ask the gods, how their eyes
Could be too blind to see.
Still, like wayward sheep,
They rush to select the next turn-key;
From the choices of shepherd
They believe were preordained.

REMEMBERING A GHOST

When you were the subject of my words,
You poured over them, until you were stumbling
drunk upon your pride.
Yet as the depths of the lines began to increase,
You claimed to find it harder to breathe;
So you scurried back to that picture perfect surface.
Never to look back,
Never again to dip your toes beneath the page.
You became a ghost...
The most beautiful coward,
These brown eyes have ever seen.
I know now that you never found what you were
looking for outside the reservoir.
And recently, you ran away again
Without saying a word;
Leaving only fumes within your wake.
I wonder if you'll ever allow yourself to admit,
That you are dying to taste,
That which you fear the most.

RITUALS OF LONELINESS

Listen as your name is fast repeated
Like incantations for a spell.
And the sweat produced in efforts
Prove the intent to cast them well.
Hands are deliberate with their movements
In attempts to conjure your return.
But when the monument is raised,
There is no doubt the fire retains its burn.
Still, you offer the sorcerer only silence
As if you were the moon in defiant phase.
Yet, when this alchemy creates explosions
I wonder if you hear me when I praise...

OVERDUE REUNION

It remains lodged inside the stone,
As the legends once foretold.
Waiting impatiently for your divine hand,
To arrive and take ahold.
For only you could ensure its release,
And wield its unbridled power.
And use it to slay our collective demons,
During each transcendent hour.
Of course, this is just a dream
Since chaos conspires to fill your days.
Still, I long for our overdue reunion;
So I can hear as this hardened blade,
Takes your breath away.

BAPTIZED IN BLUE

After you kissed me with those perfect lips,
The rest of the world was lost to me.
Do you remember how I would stare into your eyes,
In an effort to find my bearings again, darling?
That was because every single time
I shared the same space with you,
It made me feel like gravity no longer applied to me.
Your love just does something to me;
I struggle to find the words...
When you would look at me,
And baptize me in those loving, blue eyes
You made my soul feel reborn.
When you smiled at me,
I longed to learn the ways
I could somehow become a better man.
And when you'd say my name, I swear
I felt like I imagined God feels during morning mass.
How do you do these things you do, my love?
And won't you return, to finally do them again?

THAT'S WHAT SHE SAID

It's been said that time is unkind to memories.
And while I know this to be true,
The frequency with which mine are recalled,
Has proven to do nothing but sharpen them.
With crystal clarity, I remember the smile
That poured across her perfect lips,
Just before she kissed me that morning.
And I recall her look of surprise,
As my hands grabbed her ass,
And proceeded to lift her off the ground.
And as long as I live,
I will never forget what she said
As she wrapped her legs around me.
Her soft hands touched my face,
And she whispered,
"Mmmm. That'll do it, baby."

WILL OLD FLAMES RISE?

On my lonely nights, I would often contemplate the
reasons for your silence.
Had you felt betrayed?
Maybe even offended, that other women had usurped
your place within my words?
Was there a tinge of envy, knowing another soul would
discover the joy you knew so well?
Were you angry that I would touch them, where no man
has since been able to reach you?
Tell me, darling, now that you have returned to me in
friendship, is there an urge to reclaim what you feel is
your rightful place?
Tell me, do these lines not still feel like waiting fuses in
your veins?
Are you not looking for a written spark? So that what
was once an old flame, may find what it needs to dance
again? For you know damn well the things we used to
do; the heights our fire used to reach!
We were the reason the very clouds were singed.
I remember the days when the gods sent the world rain,
just to cool us off!
I know that you have not forgotten that, my love. So tell
me, has the day finally come that you have tired of
merely existing, and wish to feel alive again?

IN MIDNIGHT SKIES

Mirror, mirror in the midnight sky.
Blind to beauty in this beholder's eye
Whilst reflecting light for mornings past
Each new phase is proof that none shall last
Still some plan their lives by stars in sight
Unaware it is you that rules their night
I have watched as you would manipulate the seas
And dance inside the minds of men with ease
Until I have found your name in both verse and prose
As if you were nothing more than a thorn-less rose
But Luna we both know your hidden truth
The darkness you have come to rule,
Is rarely understood by youth.
Still they will come to worship as you wane
Forgetting that your windows only come with pain
I pray that you will release your hold on all of us,
For it is only when you drive the sun away,
That you will beg mortals for their trust.

AND SO WE REACH THE END...

"Resistance to revelation, resistance to becoming conscious of all that dwells within us - high and low, light and dark - is the anti-change factor. It is also the mainspring of all our psychological fears."

- Guy Finley

"All writing is that structure of revelation. There's something you want to find out. If you know everything up front in the beginning, you really don't need to read further if there's nothing else to find out."

- *Walter Mosley*

LETTERS FROM THE BELL TOWER

The world rarely reaches me here within the tower.
From this window, I have witnessed
the passing of people young and old;
all carrying on about their lives.
From this tower, I have released these written letters
as if they were flowers;
Aiming to give something beautiful
to the occasional maiden whom would
pass this prison and glance upward.
Even this far from the ground,
I could honestly feel their curious gaze;
and with each look it reminded me of a time I felt alive.
And so, in my misplaced zeal,
I would reach out for them; as if they were a lifeline.
Yet to my dismay, I would find
their boundaries cemented well in place.
Their gorgeous faces decorated
with an unmistakable indifference;
and their perfect lips were generous
with a silence thicker than the morning fog.
But such is life for the beast whom rings the bell;
and it is further proof
that I have nothing left to offer these maidens.
A mind once filled with brilliance,
now breeds only anger and resentment.
The fire within, that once burned
and nearly consumed a Queen,
has long since extinguished.
A sword once proudly wielded,
now lies firmly lodged within its stone.
I fear I am to die alone inside these walls.
Worse yet I fear it shall matter to no one...
Not even the crows.
And so I believe even the gods would decree:
"This tower must come down!"
Thus, I will burn it to the ground.
For this tower has become a noose,

and my legs will swing no longer.
I will rebuild myself.
Into something better,
Into someone stronger.

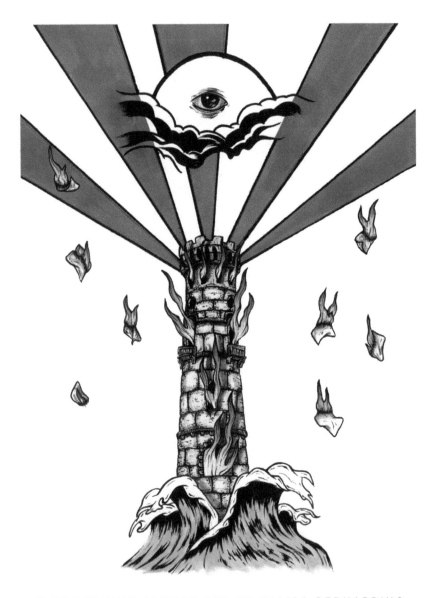

"THE BURNING TOWER" ART BY VALISA BERNARDINO

"Destruction, hence, like creation
Is one of Nature's mandates."
- *Marquis De Sade*

CLYDE HURLSTON

Lightning Source UK Ltd.
Milton Keynes UK
UKHW020944050921
389938UK00006B/147